An Uncommon Cancer Journey

To Vic,
One of my most
favorite friends, with
thanks for your wisdom
and skill.

Love,
Alice

Praise for
An Uncommon Cancer Journey

Marriage and cancer take both partners on a journey in which survival of the marriage and surviving cancer are both uncertainties. In this emotionally honest memoir, Alice Hardesty writes about the two successive terminal diagnoses that her husband survived and the wide range of therapies tried: conventional with chemo, surgery, and radiation, mind-body-spirit, spiritual-psychic, and various alternative treatments, as well as individual, couples, and group psychotherapy. Just as it helps to read about what other travelers, pilgrims, or explorers encounter when venturing into the unknown, so it can for those who find themselves on a cancer journey.

—JEAN SHINODA BOLEN, M.D.
Jungian Analyst and author, *Goddesses in Every Woman,*
and *Close to the Bone: Cancer as a Soul Journey,* among others.
Her latest book is *Artemis: The Indomitable Spirit in Everywoman.*

๛

My experience and my belief is that cancer often is a "soul event." Alice Hardesty's book offers us such a good example of how that looks in real life. She writes about their "amazing physical healing amid the interplay of emotional and spiritual forces" with refreshing honesty. Her story is compelling, illustrating what extraordinary experiences ordinary people can have.

—JAN ADRIAN
Executive Director of Healing Journeys
and founder of the conferences:
Cancer as a Turning Point, From Surviving to Thriving.

๛

An Uncommon Cancer Journey is an unusual memoir about a subject that has been written about quite often. What makes it unique is not only the outcome for the author's very sick husband, but the journey through which they both travel—from conventional medicine to alternative treatment, to even more far-out alternative treatment; a spiritual journey from western to eastern, from fear and resignation to hope and persistence. From the author's regular acupressure treatments on her husband's body to the intense therapy through which they heal an almost-broken marriage, this story is written with such remarkable clarity and honesty that readers will accept, and perhaps even want to pursue, roads to healing that are open to the truly open-minded.

—JUDITH BARRINGTON
Poet and memoirist, author of several books, including *Writing the Memoir: From Truth to Art*. She is presently completing her fourth collection of poems, *The Conversation*.

Alice Hardesty makes it very clear that anyone on a cancer journey—patients or family caregivers—cannot remain unchanged. That wake-up call challenges and changes who we are, what matters to us, the depth of our relationships, even our view and understanding of life itself. We become more authentic, stronger than we knew, and more open to life's possibilities and deeper dimensions.

There is no guidebook for any individual path. This book is the author's unflinchingly honest personal story of her husband's diagnosis, their search for treatments, his recovery from a deadly illness, and both of their healing. Readers learn the three things she says she wants us to know: that caregivers have emotions they feel they shouldn't be having; that people even with the worst kinds of cancer can be cured, sometimes in non-traditional ways; and that a crushing blow of fate—"a cosmic kick"—can bring unexpected and profound gifts.

—RUTH BOLLETINO, PH.D.,
Co-Director of Cancer as a Turning Point—
Mind-Body Psychotherapy and Counseling,
Author, *How to Talk with Family Caregivers about Cancer*

AN UNCOMMON CANCER JOURNEY

The Cosmic Kick That Healed Our Lives

ALICE HARDESTY

Bacho Press

PORTLAND, OREGON

DEDICATION

To the memory of Jack,
with unending gratitude
for his courage, loyalty,
and steadfast love.

ACKNOWLEDGMENTS

Many friends have helped with the long gestation of this book. My Ashland writing group listened on a weekly basis for a year as the story initially unfolded. Later, my Portland writing group provided encouragement as it developed further. I am indebted to my early readers, Liz Vesecky and Nancy Nowak, for their helpful suggestions. Thanks go to Ann Eames for some very useful editing, and to Maureen R. Michelson, who provided not only an editor's pencil but also the impetus to dig deeply and be vulnerable. For invaluable instruction in the craft of memoir, I am indebted to Judith Barrington, and for sensitive advice on the manuscript to Ruth Gundle.

The painting "Tumbler" used for the cover art, is the work of Jon Leach and Holly Warner. This painting and its title seem to fit the story as well as the sensibilities of both Jack and me. We carried Jon's work in our gallery in Ashland, and Jack and Jon were close friends. Special thanks to book designer Sherry Wachter for her patience and flexibility in designing the book cover and interior.

Much gratitude goes to the friends who helped me return home so suddenly from England when Jack died: the Tyndale-Biscoes in England, Liz and Al Dosa in San Francisco, and John Stromberg in Ashland. Thanks also to the many friends who brought meals, sent flowers, wrote letters, left candles on the doorstep, and reminded me of the love we shared with the Ashland community. Finally, my deep appreciation and affection go to Marianne and Rob Hardesty for standing by their dad and me all these years.

CONTENTS

PREFACE

I remember the days when cancer was almost synonymous with death. People were so fearful that they hesitated to talk about it. One friend wouldn't use the word in front of her children, so she said Aunt Dorothy had the "big C." Nowadays, cancer is depressingly common, but fortunately treatable, and often curable.

However, to this day there are certain types of cancer, esophageal being one, that are still deadly. The story of my husband's recovery from esophageal cancer in the 1980s is an exception, even thirty years later. When doctors diagnosed Jack with esophageal cancer, we began a journey that employed every technique available—traditional as well as alternative. One of them, or a combination of them, worked. Exactly which one or ones, we'll never know. What I do know is that Jack overcame two "terminal" diagnoses and went on to live another twenty years, healthy and happy.

This is the story of an amazing physical healing amid the interplay of emotional and spiritual forces. In the end, healing happened for both of us on many levels. The healing of our relationship is the more difficult one to talk about, and as a consequence, the hand-written draft of this manuscript in its cardboard folder followed me from place to place for several years, untouched.

In addition to Jack's healing, I experienced healing on this journey as well. My story includes self-revelations that I'm not proud of, along with ordinary episodes of a troubled marriage. I was reluctant to admit how fearful and angry I was that my husband was threatening to check out on me; angry that he was getting so much attention and nobody was doting on me—much harder to admit. I also had to admit that I was angry that Jack was paying full alimony and child support to his former wife when he couldn't afford to pay for his own cancer treatment. While writing this memoir, I considered leaving out the unpleasant and embarrassing details, but I believe it is important for the reader to know about my less than heroic behaviors. In our culture it is completely unacceptable to be angry or mean with a person struggling with a terminal illness. And yet, it is understandable.

So, I have pulled together the courage to write this book in hopes that both the cancer patients and care-givers who read it will know at least three things: They are not the only caregivers with socially unacceptable emotions; people with the worst kinds of cancers can be healed, even in non-traditional ways; and fate can sometimes deal us a terrible hand, which can actually turn out to be a miraculous blessing.

Life-threatening illness has been likened to the journey through a labyrinth, for the caregivers and loved ones, as well as for the patient. You can be pretty sure how you got in, and sometimes you're just thrust in, but it's not at all clear how you're going to get out. I have learned that in the process of navigation, it becomes all about the journey rather than the destination.

—ALICE HARDESTY

In a dark time,
the eye begins to see.

—THEODORE ROETHKE

CHAPTER ONE
Swallowing

There's a theory that any physical ailment has a psychological counterpart. So pains in the neck and shoulders could be related to feelings of carrying a heavy burden, or a headache could represent doubt or conflict. With Jack, it was difficulty swallowing.

Jack's job at the National Institute for Occupational Safety and Health in Washington, D.C. had become a source of intense frustration. Shortly before our marriage in 1980, Jack's boss and friend, whom he greatly admired, had been fired as a result of political shenanigans and replaced by a man Jack didn't respect. After about a year, Jack's new boss transferred him to the Office on Smoking and Health, known as "the Smoke House," where he worked in public relations. But the Reagan administration had just come into power, and the program staff was not allowed to say anything that would antagonize the tobacco industry. They couldn't report the research results honestly, and much to Jack's chagrin, were not allowed to say that smoking was addictive. Elsewhere in the government, the staff couldn't even use the word "cancer." All of this was very hard for Jack to swallow.

As a younger man, Jack and his brother Bob had worked in the Lyndon Johnson Administration. Jack and I had always admired President Johnson, except for his tragic decisions on Vietnam. Bob had been Johnson's speechwriter, and Jack had been to the White House more than once. During the Johnson presidency, Jack had worked for the Public Health Service, where he became a champion for American workers. He had collaborated with a team of health professionals and union members to create and publicize the first major study of coal miner's black lung disease. Their efforts were largely responsible for the Federal Coal Mine Safety and Health Act of 1969. Shortly after that, Jack had worked for a congressional committee and, with his brother, helped draft another piece of landmark legislation: the Occupational Safety and Health Act of 1970. The OSHA Act ordered the protection of more than twenty million Americans against workplace diseases and injuries. But by 1981, the glory days were over.

At the Smoke House, Jack had worked to create public service ads about the evils of smoking, targeting children and young adults. He once described his work there as "going after a tank [the tobacco industry] with a pea-shooter." Somehow, he never seemed to make the connection between his mission at the Smoke House and the fact that he had smoked a pipe for many years, and sometimes cigars. He had quit the pipe a few years earlier, but he still liked an occasional cigar. He was convinced that cigarette smoking was the major culprit, addictive and deadly, pushed on the American public by an unscrupulous industry.

At one point, his office contracted with an agency that used the young Brooke Shields in a very effective ad. Brooke would toss her head of glossy hair and say sweetly how she hated smelly cigarette smoke around her because she'd just have to wash her hair again. The White House nixed the ad, calling Brooke Shields, who had recently starred in *Blue Lagoon,* "anti-family." Brooke's mother had told her, "Don't worry, dear. The President will intervene because, after all, he was an actor, too." Of course, Reagan never intervened, and the ad was rejected. But Jack and his colleagues gave it to the Lung Association, which aired it as their own public service ad. And then Jack quit.

Jack's purgatory in the Smoke House was thankfully short-lived because he got his job abolished with the help of some colleagues. This meant he had the option of retiring from the federal government with a small pension, even though he was only fifty-three. He jumped at the chance. Within a few months, Jack found a job as a laborer with Custom Crafters, a high-end construction company. He was a happy man driving a dump truck while smoking cigarillos and listening to his favorite tapes of Duke Ellington and the Ink Spots. The extent of his joy in such a menial job underscored the intensity of his hatred for what the government had become. The causes he fought for over the decades—the environment, public health, and occupational health and safety—were all being trashed. It was 1981, the beginning of the Reagan Administration's systematic dismantlement of social programs.

About that time, I happened to watch a PBS special about a province in Northwest China that had an unusually high rate of esophageal cancer—fifty times greater than the rest of the world. Barefoot doctors and scientists were dispatched to the area to try to figure out the causes. Evidently the soil in that part of the country contained traces of nitrosamines and fungal contaminants, and it was devoid of certain nutrients. Also, there was a local practice of eating a rough, spiny pickle, which abraded the esophagus. That, coupled with low levels of the antioxidant vitamin C, caused a significantly high rate of esophageal cancer. The presenting symptom was always difficulty swallowing.

That information was like a bolt of lightning. Suddenly, I knew—not just suspected—why Jack had been making some strange faces at the dinner table recently. When I had asked him about it, he just passed it off, saying, "I just had trouble swallowing that particular bite." But it happened with many particular bites. I told him about the TV program and my concern, and he agreed to make an appointment with my doctor. (At that time he didn't even have his own physician.) Then, without waiting for Jack to make the call, I made an appointment for him and told Dr. Alpert's receptionist it was urgent.

Three days later, Dr. Alpert examined Jack. I had suggested that Jack ask the doctor if it could be due to stress. Dr. Alpert's reply had been, "Your wife, maybe, but not you—you're too relaxed."

Jack reported this interaction with some degree of amusement. "Not funny," I said. But it foreshadowed a role that I was to play from then on, to the immense good fortune and simultaneous frustration of us both: the dual role of loving helpmate and controlling bitch. Although that dichotomy was a source of angst at the time, later, I could look back on my controlling role and see it more like the tenacious, determined, and sometimes fierce protector. And occasionally, I was just a bitch!

Dr. Alpert made an appointment for Jack to have an x-ray. Sure enough, he had a mass on his esophagus. A needle biopsy confirmed that it was a malignant tumor. Fortunately, Dr. Alpert's colleague, Dr. Gold, had connections at the National Cancer Institute of the National Institutes of Health (NIH), and he was able to get Jack admitted to an experimental program to treat esophageal cancer. Not so fortunately, the doctors who were to treat Jack had a medical meeting in Chicago and wouldn't get him started in the program for two more weeks. Those were two of the longest weeks of my life.

In those first few weeks after the diagnosis, my state of mind alternated between anxiety and dread. I knew that the prognosis for esophageal cancer was poor. Dr. Gold told us that Jack's five-year survival chances were about fifty percent. Later, I read in a medical textbook that the chances were more like zero percent. Often, I burst into tears at the dinner table, watching TV, or in the middle of the night. Jack, who was always much more sanguine about the whole situation than I, finally told me gently that I had said all those sad things and cried all those tears before, and asked me if I would please stop.

In early October, about six weeks after I had watched the fateful TV program on esophageal cancer in China, Jack was admitted to NIH and started the experimental program of chemotherapy and eventual surgery. He was given an intravenous mixture of chemicals: cisplatin, vindesine, and bleomycin. Of the three, cisplatin was the most aggressive, and the doctors told us that one of the side effects could be deafness, which I found very disturbing. Another of the possible side effects was death, and they had us sign a statement that absolved the NIH of responsibility in that eventuality. Of course, we understood the effect of no treatment would also be death, and that loomed a lot more certain than the dangers associated with chemotherapy. So, we signed, and Jack opened his veins to the powerful cocktail.

CHAPTER TWO
A Less Than Perfect Marriage

Jack and I had known each other for almost ten years before we married, most of that time as friends and professional colleagues. At one point, I was living in Ohio working on my doctoral dissertation when I heard that Jack and his wife, Margot, had separated. When I got back to Washington, I called him up and we started seeing each other socially. After several months, casual dating turned into romance, and then things started moving fast.

I had just turned forty and decided that it might be time to finally settle down, and Jack was about ready for a serious partner after playing the field for a couple of years. We were a good match: We were attracted to each other, and we shared educated, liberal, middle-class values as well as our Midwest heritage. We loved to talk politics, enjoyed partying, and drank a lot. In fact, he drank a great deal more than I did, but drinking was a big part of my life as well. I remember thinking at the time we started dating that I had never met a person who could drink so much and yet hold it so well. Jack had the proverbial hollow leg, and my admiration was mixed with only a small portion of apprehension.

Jack was a bit unconventional, both in appearance and attitude. Medium-tall and slight of build, his curly hair and luxuriant mustache were a rich dark brown. He wore glasses that turned dark in the sunlight, so the blue of his eyes was only noticeable indoors. Always the natty dresser, he had strong opinions about what colors went together, and I learned not to make recommendations. He would often top off his outfit with a hat—anything from a Greek fisherman's cap to a bowler. My mother never quite understood Jack's wry sense of humor and his lack of interest in conventional small talk. Yet, she was happy that at my advanced age I was finally settling down with a respectable man. She accepted our relationship even before we were married.

Soon after our romance started, we decided to move in together. We picked out a house in the D.C. suburb of Silver Spring, where I moved, and he was to follow as soon as his divorce was final. That process dragged on for six more months, and eventually, he moved in as well. The next year or so was like a honeymoon with trips to Greece and Italy. Finally, we decided to get married, or more accurately, I persuaded Jack to marry me. He reluctantly agreed even though he was having a fine time living in unmarried bliss and was in no hurry to try the conventional thing again. However, I longed for the status and security of marriage and knew I would feel more comfortable with my parents' visits if we formalized our relationship. In future years, when Jack wanted to blame me for our dysfunctional relationship, he would say that I only married him to please my parents. As is often the case, there was some truth to that.

On April 12, 1980, we were married at home in a small ceremony. Instead of the joyous celebration I had always imagined my wedding would be, we both spent the day worrying about how his children, Marianne, twelve, and Robert, ten, would accept our marriage. For quite a while, they were well aware of the seriousness of our relationship and had lived with us part time for much of the previous eighteen months. Still, we worried. Like many other young children, they must have hoped that their parents would eventually reunite. On a deeper level, Jack and I worried about how we would take this new commitment to each other and to the institution of marriage. It seemed as if all the unacknowledged emotional baggage began unpacking itself, and we began tripping over it on our wedding day.

It's hard to say exactly what was happening between us. Nothing was working out the way I had expected. I didn't feel more secure, and the simple gold wedding band that Jack bought for me didn't really add to my status. Jack was suffering delayed remorse about leaving his family, even though his former wife, Margot, had actually kicked him out of the house in anger and frustration at his lack of emotional support just two years prior to our moving in together. We saw his children regularly, as they came to our house on Wednesday evenings and weekends. Jack had made a generous settlement agreement with Margot, giving her the house in Bethesda, plenty of financial support for the kids, and lifetime alimony. Later on, after Jack left his government job, the alimony would become a serious bone of contention when his illness claimed so much of our resources.

Jack was feeling tremendous guilt, not only for leaving Margot and the kids, but also about the death of his eldest son, Sturges, who died several years earlier of nephritis at age nine. Although Jack rarely spoke about him, I knew this unresolved grief weighed heavily. While we were still dating, I had asked him about what went wrong with his marriage. Jack replied that he had been "out to lunch," and while Sturges was dying and Margot desperately needed Jack's support, he was either at the office or under his car. That was when Jack was working in a congressional office, swept up in the excitement of drafting legislation, and drinking heavily.

During the first year of our marriage, I was unaware of the causes of my unhappiness, except that I felt disappointed and left out. Jack and the kids would take long bike rides that exceeded my stamina, and they seemed to like their dad's cooking better than mine (perfectly understandable in retrospect). They were a family that I was not a part of, at least not yet, and I wasn't sure if I ever would be. It was not until several months after our marriage when Margot decided to move with the kids to Florida that I realized they had become an important part of my life. I broke down in tears at the idea that they would be so far from their father, and also from me. In the end, this would not be a lengthy separation, since they were all back within a year.

More disturbing to me was all the time Jack spent doing things for Margot, which only increased after our wedding. It seemed like he was always talking to her at length on the phone, helping her with chores, driving the kids around, even helping Margot's mother move to a different apartment. One time, I called him at work and left a message for him to call his wife. He told me later that he didn't know whether he should call me—or Margot.

All the while, alcohol conveniently masked our emotions—his guilt about his family and his unhappiness with his work, and my disappointment and frustrations with the marriage. Since I was still working in my government job at the Occupational Safety and Health Administration (OSHA), I traveled quite a bit and attended professional meetings out of town, even abroad. Within a few months of our wedding, I rekindled an affair with a colleague, a relationship I had ended when the romance with Jack had begun back in 1977. Now, I had something to feel guilty about. In fact, I was horribly conflicted. Each time I returned home, I would vow *never* to give in to this other man again; then each time I would see him at a meeting I would slide back into his embrace. *Here is somebody who really appreciates me,* I told myself.

Later, when Jack and I were in counseling, our therapist would say, "Affairs are so easy. You're together for a weekend, you have great sex, and then you go home. No laundry, no kids, no responsibilities. They're just not real at all."

My affair was a dirty secret, and I wore it like a hair shirt, alternating between being extra nice to Jack and hating him, all the while hating myself. In the evening, alcohol deadened the pain temporarily, but by morning it was back again. I started to see a counselor, who was only marginally helpful, but she prescribed an antidepressant that at least put an end to my insomnia. Later, when we started seeing Barbara, a truly effective dragon-lady of a therapist, I realized the antidepressant, like the alcohol, only served further to mask the problems and helped me avoid dealing with the root of my depression.

One fine autumn weekend about six months after we were married, we took a day-trip to a river in western Maryland to picnic and swim. The leaves were beginning to turn gold, and yet, the air still held the softness of summer. Jack was always a strong swimmer, and despite the swift, cold current, made his way easily to an island in the center of the river. I jumped in to follow and quickly felt the current pulling me downstream. I summoned the Australian crawl I'd excelled at as a teenager to take me on the diagonal toward the island. As I fought my way toward Jack, I was nearly overwhelmed by the larger struggle that was consuming my life. A part of me wanted just to let go and be swept away, while another part wanted desperately to be at his side. After what felt like a superhuman effort, I reached the island, trembling and unable to stand as he pulled me out.

A year later, when the cancer came along, the distraction was sufficient to put aside my desires for infidelity, as well as our unspoken disappointments and frustrations—at least temporarily. We now had a common enemy, one that we would fight to the death.

CHAPTER THREE

Chemo

Jack started chemotherapy as an inpatient at the NIH about three weeks after his initial diagnosis. He tolerated it remarkably well, enduring only mild nausea at times. Because they had to keep careful track of his urinary output, he had to wear a Foley catheter, which Jack considered the worst part of the treatment. Wherever Jack went, the catheter had to go. During the several weeks of his treatment, he received chemotherapy about three hours every day, at which time he was a prisoner of I.V. tubes and bags, as well as the catheter.

As the treatment continued, Jack's thick dark hair began to fall out in clumps. One day he went into the bathroom, shaved his head, and emerged bald. He seemed proud that he had managed to do it by himself, and perhaps a bit pleased at the anticipated shock value. Although I had routinely cut his hair, I had not offered to do this. The aspect of shaving off his beautiful, thick hair and turning him into an obviously sick person was too depressing. I appreciated Jack's courage, but I was saddened by how thin and vulnerable he looked.

Despite the discomfort and the grim prognosis, Jack's spirits remained high. He was always cheerful when I arrived to visit, and with the medical staff he was cooperative and pragmatic. He liked them all and appreciated their efficient care, especially his nurse, Margaret Flanagan, with whom he later corresponded for several years. His friends marveled at his optimistic attitude.

Years later, Jack told us that he just decided he would probably get through all of this alright and if he didn't, that would be how it would be. He would tell himself: *If the cancer takes over and threatens my life, well, I'll cross that bridge when I get to it.*

I believe this attitude served him very well over the next few years. Some of our friends insisted that Jack was in denial, which proved to be at least partially true in some aspects of his self-care. Now, I see it as a firm and nonaggressive way of saying, "This thing is not going to get the better of me!"

Most of the rest of us, however, were not nearly so cheerful. Several of Jack's old friends came to visit him before Christmas, including a contingent from Provincetown, where he had vacationed often with his family, and later with me. They undoubtedly thought it was the last time they would see him. That Christmas his brother Bob sent him a beautiful pair of custom-made, hand-tooled, Texan cowboy boots that must have cost at least $500. I remember thinking, *That's a dumb present; spending all that money on something Jack will have little use for because we all know he's going to die.*

Actually, Jack loved those boots, and ultimately, wore them for nearly twenty-five years!

Jack's kids visited him sporadically in the hospital. Robert, who was twelve at the time, hated all the tubes and the smell of illness, which both kids had probably experienced during their brother's fatal illness several years earlier. I imagine it was frightening for them to be faced with the possible death of their father, especially when they were so young. Plus, the loss of Jack's thick curly hair and his beautiful mustache, combined with his thin body, didn't do much to promote optimism on our part. (Oddly, when his hair grew back after chemotherapy, it was straight. Then, a few years later, after another regimen of chemotherapy, it grew back curly.)

One unsuspected source of support for me was Margot, who at that time worked in the library at NIH. When I visited Jack, I would usually stop to see her, and we would compare notes about his treatment and morale. We would also start talking about Jack the person, his idiosyncrasies, and what it was like when Margot and Jack were married. These conversations were always enlightening. We had not had much contact prior to this time, and we joked about how Jack had kept us apart because he was afraid we would gang up on him. My friendship with Margot, even though strained at times, would endure, and I still look back on those moments with gratitude.

My memory of my own response during these months is blurred. I do remember feeling anxiety, which I dealt with by planning. For example, if Jack died, which I pretty much expected him to do, I would sell our house in Silver Spring and move back to my old apartment condo in D.C. that I still owned. Possibly, I would go back to work for the government since I had earlier quit my job at OSHA and had opened my own consulting practice. Perhaps I would join the Sierra Club to meet new men. Whether or not I would jump back into the affair was an open question, but I would certainly continue going to professional meetings.

At that time, I didn't even dwell on how long Jack would live or what we would do to salvage our marriage if he lived a long time. Even though I remained hopeful that the treatment would work, I felt I needed to plan for the worst.

Although I was seeing a counselor during Jack's treatment, I remember very little about those sessions. It was as if the dysfunctional aspects of our marriage, coupled with a life-threatening illness, were so overwhelming that I was reluctant to deal with them. I was completely numb to my own emotions. So, I made the expected daily visits to the hospital, immersed myself in my consulting practice, and left the necessary emotional and spiritual work until later.

At one point, Jack and I felt that we needed some cheer in our lives and we decided to get a dog. The only breed that we readily agreed upon was a yellow Labrador retriever. We had seen yellow Labs in London and noticed how beautiful and well behaved they were. We had seen them in pubs or under tables in restaurants, lying at their masters' feet. There was a pet store not far from us that specialized in breeding Labs and great Danes, so I called them up. It just so happened that the storeowner had recently adopted an eight-week-old puppy, the pick of the litter, that she no longer wanted. The woman was newly pregnant and decided there would be more than enough baby energy in the house. A puppy would be just too much. We asked if we could "look at" the puppy.

Jack had always advocated meeting a dog's parents, so we did make the acquaintance of the father, a dignified black Lab who approached and leaned against anyone who spoke to him. After this peaceful introduction, the owner let loose her "pup-pup," a whirling dervish of little paws and kisses. We ended up taking her home and we all fell in love with her immediately. It was impossible not to be cheered by such a lively and affectionate spirit. When nobody could think of just the right name, Jack finally named her Patty-Laverne-Maxine after the Andrews Sisters, and henceforth, she was known as Max. For nearly fourteen years, Max would be an important member of our family.

CHAPTER FOUR
Surgery

About a month after the beginning of chemotherapy, Jack had a CT scan. To everybody's amazement, the large tumor that the doctors had declared inoperable had shrunk to a fraction of its original size. That good news allowed us to experience Christmas with a sense of optimism, although more treatment waited in the New Year.

The next milestone in Jack's treatment was surgery, scheduled for mid-January. The surgical team planned to remove his entire esophagus, pull up his stomach, which they described as "just a floppy sack," and attach it to the back of his nasopharynx. That meant he would then swallow directly into his stomach.

A couple of days before the surgery, Frank Schaeffer, one of Jack's friends from Provincetown, arrived to give us support. I'm sure he thought, as quite a few did, that Jack might not make it through this long and complex surgery.

Once Jack was back in the hospital, Frank, a recovering alcoholic, took the opportunity to make his pitch to me. "Jack's an alcoholic, you know."

My first response was to defend Jack, justifying my own indifference to the matter. "No, he's not. He's given up martinis."

"Yes, but he still drinks wine, and a lot of it."

"Sure, but wine's not bad," I countered. "Besides, he's given up cigars, too."

"Doesn't matter. Once an alcoholic always an alcoholic," Frank declared. "He needs to give it up completely."

After that conversation, I thought, *Just what I need, another person pushing on me in an already stressful situation.*

In fact, Jack's old boss, Jack Finklea, a brilliant physician and beloved friend, had told us that esophageal cancer was often called "bartender's disease" after the guys who always had a cigarette going and a shot of whiskey just behind the bar. Evidently, the incidence of esophageal cancer for those who both drank and smoked was sixty-five times greater than for those who didn't. For some reason, nature neglected to give the esophagus a protective mucous membrane lining. Alcohol, which is absorbed immediately into the bloodstream as it courses down the esophagus, stresses the sensitive tissues. Then, small amounts of ingested nicotine and tar abrade the tissues and compound the problem.

"Okay," I assured Frank, "I'll mention it to his doctor."

"I think you should tell him yourself," Frank persisted.

A lot of good that would do, I told myself.

Jack's surgery was scheduled for 8:00 a.m. and I knew it was going to be a long operation, at least six hours. So, I slept like a baby with the help of the antidepressant, and went over to NIH with Frank around 10:30 that morning. It didn't even occur to me that there could have been life-and-death questions that the surgeons might need to ask me. What if his heart had stopped during the operation? What if he had suffered brain damage? Should they continue? Later, I was appalled at my apathetic behavior.

Reflecting on that time, I now see myself enveloped by a cloud of denial—a great fog, like being in a dream. Oblivious to the stark realities of the situation, I was unable to access my own feelings. I try not to judge myself, as it seems to have been a survival mechanism, the way some people deal with abuse by denying that it exists. I now have a better understanding of my ambivalence during Jack's conventional treatment. I felt as though I had absolutely no control over anything.

Jack stayed in the hospital for ten days recovering from the surgery. Once again, the medical staff was thrilled by how rapidly he healed and what a cooperative patient he was. The surgery was more radical than I had imagined. During the eight-hour process, the doctors had broken two of Jack's ribs and removed another so the surgeons could reach the esophagus.

When I had the opportunity to see Jack's torso post surgery, it was clear they had indeed laid him open. A massive scar stretched from his upper chest all the way down his right side and into his back. There were additional incisions, including a round one on his side for a feeding tube that was later withdrawn because it never really worked. Those surgical scars, like battle scars or warrior wounds frightened me at first, but later became dear to me. After Jack healed, sometimes I would run my fingers over them, full of awe and gratitude for the doctors, for Jack's courage, and for the Universe that had cooperated in his healing.

During the surgery, the doctors intubated Jack with a respirator that remained in place for two days to help him breathe. When I arrived the day a technician was going to remove the respirator, Jack was angry for the first (and only) time during the whole course of his treatment at NIH. The respirator was still in place, so he couldn't talk. He signaled for pen and paper, and when I asked how he was, he wrote, "Mad!"

"What's the problem?" I asked.

He scribbled, "The technician, she treats me like a child!"

"What did she do?"

"Talks down to me. I didn't do it right, so she went away!"

Evidently, Jack had ordered her away. Later, she returned and they completed the procedure successfully.

Afterward, when people expressed sympathy for all the, pain Jack endured—the toxic chemotherapy, the nausea, the fear he must have felt—he would say that the only parts he really minded were the respirator and the Foley catheter. Not only was the catheter uncomfortable, but it felt like he was imprisoned by a chain leading from his penis to a big sack hanging from a nearby coat rack. Not a very happy condition for a man who liked to think of himself as rich, handsome, and well informed. (At least handsome and well informed.)

After the surgery, I finally did corner Jack's physician, Dr. Jack Roth, whom Jack liked and respected. I asked him if quite a few of his patients had been drinkers, and he replied in the affirmative.

"Did they give it up after the treatment?" I continued.

"Well, no. Most of them just drank more."

This could be one reason, I later reflected, why the protocol seemed to have failed for the other patients.

Dr. Roth did agree to talk to Jack about the benefits of not drinking. Each day, I asked Jack if Dr. Roth had given him any advice about anything, and the answer was always *no*—until the last day. Dr. Roth came into Jack's room to say goodbye and wish him well. Then, when he was almost out the door, he mumbled, "By the way, it'd be better not to drink too much, and if I were you, I'd give it up completely." So much for bedside counseling.

While Jack's recuperation felt like an eternity to him, the doctors thought it was exceptionally fast. Soon, he was home, feeling energetic and eager to get back to his construction job.

Over the next six months, Jack went back to NIH every week because he had, by a roll of the dice, become part of a group that would receive additional chemotherapy. Half the subjects in the protocol received it, and the other half went without. It turns out that there were precancerous spots all up and down his extracted esophagus, so the additional chemo was probably a good idea. I would have preferred him to be done with it, at least in part, because, once again, the doctors told him that he might lose his hearing. This was one of the first protocols ever to use cisplatin, known from animal experiments to damage the sensory cells of the inner ear. But the doctors didn't just say Jack might lose some hearing; they told me that he might "go deaf." As an audiologist with degrees in deaf education as well as audiology, I damn well knew the difference between hearing loss, which can be any degree of mild-to-severe, and deafness, which effectively puts an end to aural communication. I wondered, *How can these doctors be so cavalier about something so serious.*

"Better than death, I suppose," was Jack's philosophy on the question.

Yes, better than death, I thought, but the prospect of having to communicate by writing everything down, of having such an impediment to intimacy, and of dealing with the inevitable loss and depression for both of us, was daunting.

What next? Would they tell me that another chemical in the cocktail would make Jack go blind? It turned out that he did, indeed, lose some hearing, but it was a relatively mild, high frequency loss, and progressed only a little as he grew older.

Another thing that the doctors fortunately got wrong was Jack's eating requirements. They said he would never again be able to eat a big meal, but would have to have five or six small meals throughout the day. He ignored that advice from the outset, and it never was a problem.

Something the doctors neglected to mention altogether was the outward appearance of his digestive process. Because the surgery took place in January and Jack was easily chilled after that, he was in the habit of wearing turtlenecks under his sweaters. When the warm weather came, we would have meals in the fresh air on the porch, and Jack started to wear shirts open at the collar. Toward the end of one such dinner, Marianne cried with alarm, "Dad, your neck!"

All eyes were riveted on an enormous bulge in Jack's neck. I rushed to the phone and called NIH. The doctor on duty at the Cancer Institute asked us to describe this bulge and then asked Jack if it hurt. On hearing that it didn't, the doctor said to call him back in the morning if it was still there. It wasn't, so we just chalked it up to another cancer treatment mystery. That evening, however, after spaghetti and meatballs, the bulge reappeared. This time I contained my hysteria and decided to check its progress every half-hour or so. At bedtime, it was mostly gone, and by morning, it had disappeared.

Evidently the doctor on duty didn't know enough about the operation to remind us that the surgeons had replaced the esophagus by pulling the stomach up to the naso-pharynx, which in effect, was in his neck. After that, we referred to it as his "tennis ball." It became such an ordi-nary fact of life that at dinner parties when his hostess would ask him if he would like second helpings, he would point to the bulge in his neck and say, "No thanks, I'm full."

CHAPTER FIVE

Remission

Jack recovered well from the radical surgery, even though it wasn't fast enough to suit him, and within a few weeks he was happy to be back to work at Custom Crafters as a cabinetmaker's assistant. The only reminder of the whole ordeal was the weekly dose of chemotherapy, which lasted about six months after his surgery.

Because we considered the cancer past history, or more likely, because we were reluctant to enter the murky waters of mortality, we had no deep conversations about death or the avoidance of death, or the opportunity for a second chance at life. Nor did we have any such conversation with the kids or our friends. All of that would come later. The next three years slid by with few distinct events. We thought Jack was cured. The doctors would say "in remission," which sounded more like a temporary reprieve. Neither of us would use the word "remission."

Post treatment, our life settled into a quiet pattern. Our marital state was not significantly improved, nor had it deteriorated. I continued to see the counselor, but she never suggested seeing us as a couple, so the level of communication between Jack and me remained superficial. Jack enjoyed his construction jobs, and I enjoyed my work as an audiology consultant, especially the traveling. Although I had sworn off my long-standing affair while Jack was going through the heroic parts of the treatment, I succumbed again two or three times a year at professional meetings or conferences. After each episode, I would return home and castigate myself for weeks, swearing that I would never do it again. Then I would not only fall into the trap again, but jump in with eyes wide open at the next chance. I realized that I was experiencing a kind of intensity and appreciation that seemed unavailable to me in my marriage.

Jack continued drinking—no more martinis, but plenty of wine. I discovered that he kept a bottle in the basement, available to him when he worked in his shop or on his car. He was also in regular contact with Margot, who called him to ask favors or advice, always talking at great length. Just as before, Jack ran errands for her and helped her with chores. One time, I became so exasperated with the situation, I just blurted out, "Why don't you just ask her to move in?"

Jack treated the question as rhetorical, not bothering to answer. Nor was there any change in their relationship. The friendship that Margot and I had developed while he was in the hospital began to cool, and we seldom communicated.

About two years after Jack's surgery, my parents spent Christmas with us. It was a relatively peaceful visit with no discussion of cancer or any other matters of substance. However, there was an accident during Christmas dinner. There were eight of us around the table, and I had to squeeze past some wall-mounted bookshelves to reach the dinner plates. In the process, I grabbed a shelf and the whole system—books, shelves, and pottery—crashed down onto my head and the table. Although nobody was hurt, and the dinner was mostly eaten by that time, I'll never forget the look of horror on my mother's face. It was not the broken dishes and the mess, but it was the possibility of injury to me that terrified her.

After Christmas my parents went to Hilton Head Island in South Carolina, intending to stay through February and avoid the worst part of the Chicago winter. Early in January my father called to say that my mother had suffered a heart attack, but there was no reason for me to come since it was very mild. I kept in touch for the next couple of days, but when her condition didn't improve, I began to worry. Finally, her doctor called and said her condition had deteriorated unexpectedly, so I flew to Savannah that afternoon. In the past, I had taken a shuttle from the airport to Hilton Head and, probably because we rely on old patterns in times of crisis, it never occurred to me to spend the extra money for a taxi. The trip seemed endless, as if we were floating through the South Carolina countryside populated by palmettos and golf courses, stopping at everybody's destination except my own. When we finally arrived at the hospital, I had cried through every one of my tissues. Just ten minutes earlier, my mother had died.

That evening, my father and I made phone calls to tell our family and a few close friends about Mother's death. Dad must have been in shock because he carried on in a very calm, pragmatic manner. Actually, the reality didn't hit him until several weeks later, after we had flown back to Chicago and buried her ashes in the first of the family plots to be occupied, and after all the family had gone home. But while we were in Hilton Head, my father was his usual highly competent self. On the other hand, I cried almost constantly and walked the beach feeling as though there was a hole in my heart, full of regret for the superficiality of our last visit, and for failing to tell my mother how much I loved her. Although I knew heart disease takes many years to develop, somehow, I felt that I had contributed to her death with my careless toppling of the bookshelf—and I longed to be forgiven.

My sense of loss was heightened after calling Jack that night. When I told him that Mother had died, there was a pause and then he replied, "Well, that's the way it goes." Stunned, I asked him to wait while I went into the bedroom and closed the door because I didn't want my father to hear.

"Have you been drinking?" I asked.

"Little wine, that's all."

"How could you say such a crass thing? *Well, that's the way it goes!* Is that all you have to say about my mother's death?"

Silence.

"Don't you ever...." *Ever what?* I thought. There was no point in continuing. I didn't finish that sentence until years later.

The next morning, I walked along the seashore feeling doubly orphaned by death on the one hand and by alcohol on the other. Moreover, it was difficult to know how much of Jack's indifference toward me was caused by alcohol and how much was reflective of his actual feelings while sober. Perhaps some of it had to do with the long unexpressed grief surrounding the death not only of his older son, Sturges, but of his own mother when Jack was only seven years old.

Our ability to communicate had become so poor that I didn't know what was due to resentment (and there was plenty of reason for it) and what was due to the numbing effect of alcohol. A few months later, we would begin to know that both resentment and alcohol were powerful contributors and that my own anger was equally destructive of our relationship.

In the meantime, we both went about our practical lives, sweeping even these traumatic moments aside, until, as Jack was fond of saying, he received his second "cosmic kick the ass."

CHAPTER SIX

It's Back

Early in 1985, more than two years after Jack's surgery, there was a telltale sign that something was not quite right. There was a weakness in his voice, especially when he was tired. Actually, his voice had never quite regained its strength after the surgery, but the doctors hadn't bothered to explain the reason. Many years later, we found out why from an ear, nose, and throat specialist in Oregon. When the surgeons had removed his esophagus, they inadvertently severed the nerve that led to his right vocal cord. The left cord had to do all the work, crossing the trachea to contact the paralyzed cord on the right. But now, his voice was noticeably weaker.

When Jack and I went to see Dr. Roth, he told us that several others in his protocol had developed the same symptom and that it was not a good sign. A subsequent x-ray showed a mass in his upper thorax that was pressing against the left vocal cord's nerve and causing the increase in weakness. This was followed by the inevitable biopsy and the inevitable delay in finding out the results. In fact, it took NIH nearly two weeks to complete the laboratory work and schedule a follow-up appointment with Dr. Roth.

In the meantime, we didn't sit around on pins and needles. We were pretty sure that the biopsy was going to yield bad news. Jack's reaction was, as it had always been, not to give up for a moment, but to try something new. So, we decided to investigate alternative medicine. Jack suggested calling his old friend, Barbara, who had been a neighbor when he, Margot, and the kids had lived in nearby Bethesda, Maryland. Barbara was a therapist. She knew Jack had been through a serious cancer challenge and she had told him that he ought to explore the reasons for his cancer, a conversation that Jack had not shared with me until Barbara told me later.

Once again, Jack left the logistics to me, and as usual, I felt there was no time to waste. I called Barbara immediately. I told her that Jack most likely had a recurrence and asked if she knew any alternative doctors in the area. She suggested a German physician, Dietmar Schildwaechter, in downtown D.C. But before I could even write down the name, she asked, "Why is he killing himself?"

Stunned, I couldn't even reply. Then she said, "Get him over here! *Now.*"

"Okay, I'll tell him," which I did immediately. Without a word, he got into his car and drove to Bethesda to see her.

Two hours later, Jack came home exhausted and relieved. In a style that soon became familiar, Barbara made Jack dive right into his stagnant emotional pool. In that first session they came up with all kinds of discoveries. They talked about how, when his mother died, no one would tell him what had happened. The adults would not let Jack and his younger brother see their mother's body. Instead, they took them out for ice cream. It was as if she just disappeared. Jack shared how he had said something hurtful to his mother before she had died, and he never had a chance to explain himself or make it right. He told Barbara about how his father had then married the proverbial wicked stepmother, and how mean she had been to the two boys. He explored his grief about the death of his own beloved son Sturges, who had died at age nine from chronic nephritis. Then, his first marriage had disintegrated, probably as a result of this tragedy. Subsequently, he stored up years of anguish.

"If I die soon," Jack admitted to me after this session with Barbara, "at least I will have gotten all of this off my chest."

Barbara had told Jack that she wanted to see me, too. Now I knew we had started along a different path.

Dr. Schildwaechter was a tall, imposing, Prussian type, but friendly enough and concerned. Even before we had the results of the biopsy, Jack and I were convinced the cancer had come back, as it had with most of the other patients in his protocol. After Jack explained the situation in some detail, Dr. Schildwaechter leaned back and said, "If I were you, I would go to the *Robert Janker Klinik* in Bonn."

Neither of us had ever heard of the Robert Janker Klinik or knew much about Bonn except that it was the capital of Germany at that time. Nor had treatment in a foreign country occurred to us, but we were open to any kind of alternative. Also, we knew there wasn't time to study a variety of different options. Dr. Schildwaechter knew the director of the clinic and offered to make the arrangements. We had no information about the kind of treatment Jack would receive, the cost of it, or how long it would take. It just seemed like the right thing to do. Within a week, Jack would be on a plane to Germany and I would follow a few days later.

Dr. Schildwaechter also prescribed several types of enzymes and freeze-dried bits of liver and glands from healthy animals, as well as several other supplements. His bill was high, but given the circumstances, we didn't pay much attention to finances at that time. Actually, my mother had left me $10,000, and we tore through the whole amount within a few months, paying for Jack's treatment, therapy, and the trip to Germany.

Before leaving for Germany, we went to NIH one last time to meet with Jack's surgeon to get the results of the biopsy. This time, Dr. Roth offered radiation as a palliative treatment; only because it would make Jack more comfortable for whatever time he had left, but not to expect a cure. Even if the tumor shrank, even if it disappeared, it would reappear somewhere else. Although no one uttered the words, it was clearly a death sentence. What Dr. Roth didn't know was that we were already on a different path.

So, I finally summoned the courage to ask Dr. Roth how long he thought Jack would live. It seemed a fair question, since he had implied that it wouldn't be very long. He hesitated, then finally answered, "Well, what have you read? Haven't you read about six months?"

What I had read was that esophageal cancer was virtually always fatal, but I hadn't read how quickly. At least now, I was reasonably confident that Jack wouldn't die on the plane.

As Dr. Roth was giving us the bad news, I was mesmerized by the decoration on his white jacket. It was the logo of the National Cancer Institute. There in bright blue embroidery sat St. George astride his blue horse, heroic in the rampant pose, his spear piercing the side of the metaphorical dragon—in this case, the crab. Even back then I understood that this was contemporary medicine's way to deal with illness, especially those illnesses involving tumors. Use every weapon in the medical armory to slay that dragon. Kill it, poison it, irradiate it, dig it out. Leave not a trace of it or the damn thing will grow back. Chemotherapy, radiation, and surgery are Western medicine's weapons of choice, regardless of how the body trembles under the assault.

No wonder so many people, including friends we later grew to know and love, died in the process of treatment.

Jack always maintained that his treatment at NIH had saved his life in that it bought him time. If he had not taken part in the earlier protocol, he wouldn't have survived long enough to participate in any alternative, gentler healing process.

We had no idea what the results of this new journey would be or, in fact, any knowledge of what the journey would entail. Traveling to the clinic in Bonn was a leap into the unknown. I didn't know whether Jack would live for years or whether he would die within six months as Dr. Roth had reluctantly predicted. He seemed fairly robust, but still, I knew so little about cancer that I didn't even know if he would survive the trip to Germany.

CHAPTER SEVEN
Off to Germany

There was so much we had to do in the few days before going to Germany. Fortunately, Barbara was able to make room for us in her busy schedule, and we saw her twice. Even though I barely knew her, somehow it seemed right to follow her advice to the letter, a practice that served us well in the coming months.

Barbara was a tall, good-looking woman in her fifties with a head of thick, wavy gray hair. It wasn't hard to imagine her as the high school cheerleader she once was. In her North Carolina drawl she said, "I think it would be a good idea for you to make an appointment for acupressure with Bonnie Pendleton. Here is her phone number." Then she handed us the phone, and expected us to dial, which is what we did. That was the way it went with Barbara. Whenever she said something was a good idea, we were to snap to and do it. We all knew that there was no time to waste.

Bonnie came to Barbara's house the next day and gave Jack an acupressure treatment. During the treatment,

Jack described sensitivity in various places on his body, and Bonnie told him that these were the locations on his meridians, or energy pathways, that corresponded to the upper thorax, the location of his tumor. Two days later on a Sunday morning, we both saw Bonnie, and she demonstrated a treatment protocol specifically for the upper thorax. She then gave me a page from an acupressure manual that she had authored. Although I started out completely naïve, with the help of her diagram I gradually became competent and ended up giving Jack an acupressure treatment every day for more than a year.

Another healing friend who came to the rescue was Donna Scheib, a speech therapist I had known for years. Donna had long been interested in alternative methods of healing, which she practiced in subtle ways with her patients, both with touch and with helpful suggestions. She came over to the house a couple of days before Jack left to give us a quick lesson in foot reflexology. When she massaged the upper part of the ball of his right foot, she noticed that it was slightly puffy. This, she told us, was the spot that corresponded to the upper thorax. She recommended that I massage this area every day, which, again, I did for more than a year, and within that period, the puffiness gradually disappeared.

We would never know the connection between acupressure and foot reflexology, and how these affected Jack's healing, which was the case with the myriad of other healing practices we used. But we did know that these treatments were very satisfying for both of us. Jack took to bodywork like a glutton for touch, and I found myself more relaxed and peaceful after every session. It was also something I could do for him, something intimate, a way that I could contribute to his healing. With both acupressure and reflexology, as with several other activities we initiated, I began to feel a modicum of control.

With last minute preparations, we had no time to search for the cheapest airfare to Germany. However, we discovered that British Air had a special standby fare to London, so we decided to try it. Jack went first because I needed to wrap up some of my consulting projects and pick out work that I could take along. He made the trek and called me from Bonn to tell me how to do it. I went to Dulles Airport in the morning to put my name on the standby list, then returned home and packed up, and went out again in the afternoon to take my chances. Actually, we followed this route several times that year and we were always able to get on board.

Upon arriving in London, we would take the train from Heathrow to Victoria station, transfer to Kings Cross, and take another train to Dover. From there, we took the hydrofoil to Oostende in Belgium, and another train through Brussels, Aachen, and Cologne, all the way to Bonn. Nowadays, it would probably be an expensive trip, but at that time the dollar was strong, almost three Deutsche marks to the dollar, and it seemed to be the cheapest way. I have to admit that despite all the worry and stress, this journey was an adventure. Both of us had always been enthusiastic travelers, and this trip was no exception.

Jack was not yet enrolled in the Janker Klinik because there were examinations and extensive paperwork to be done before they could decide on his protocol and start his treatment as an inpatient. At first, we stayed at the Muskowitz, a little hotel, or more accurately, a guesthouse, about a block from the clinic. We dubbed it the "cowboy" hotel because its owner loved paraphernalia from the American West. He drove an old Mustang with steer horns mounted on the hood. Our other nickname for it was "the morgue" because, despite the owner's flamboyant taste in cars and accessories, the place was the epitome of German austerity. The rooms were small and Spartan, and in the breakfast room loomed an enormous grandfather clock, whose loud tick was the only sound. Guests who ate breakfast there spoke in whispers, and the glum matron who served us hardly uttered a word. Later, we moved to livelier quarters.

Bonn was nothing like I had imagined. Even though I had been to a conference in the quaint town of Freiburg seven years earlier, I still imagined Germany's capital city to be cold and drab, the result of rebuilding after the devastation of Allied bombing during World War II. But instead of gray concrete hulks, I found charming 18th-century buildings, many of them with modern interiors behind the traditional facades. We found a book with pictures of the city before, during, and after the war. The ragged skeletons of buildings and piles of rubble seemed completely hopeless. Yet, the residents rebuilt it within a period of only ten years with great tenacity and generous support from the Marshall Plan. And they didn't go for Walter Gropius or Mies van der Rohe modernity, but rebuilt what they already knew and loved, from stately Baroque to rustic timber-framed.

The Janker Klinik, then located on Baumschulestrasse (literally Tree School Street), was more like a large house than a hospital. Certainly, it had none of the slick furnishings of modern hospitals. The floors were linoleum, the walls whitewashed, and there was no waiting room, only some benches placed here and there along the walls. It smelled faintly medicinal, but not overwhelmingly so.

Once the doctors determined a protocol for Jack, he moved into the clinic. A tiny elevator carried us to the third floor, where Jack shared a large room with three other men. As we walked down the hall, we passed a woman wearing a pink chenille bathrobe and a turban wrapped around what must have been her bald head. With one hand she pushed an I.V. pole bearing her chemotherapy bag, its umbilical cord attached to her arm. In the other, she held a bottle of beer. She was returning from the machine down the hall that rolled out bottles of good German lager when you put two marks into the slot. Quite a change from the National Institutes of Health!

After I had inspected Jack's room and said, *"Guten Tag"* to each of his roommates, we decided to go out for a walk. It was Sunday, so there would be no treatment, and he was eager to show me the city.

For a capital city, Bonn had a surprisingly provincial feeling. Fortunately, all the big, impersonal government buildings were built in Bad Godesberg, fifteen miles away. Evidently, both Berlin and Frankfurt had vied for the status of the nation's capital after World War II, so the new parliament selected Bonn, a sleepy Rhine town, half way between the two. Besides, there were the obvious complications with Berlin, partitioned into four international sectors at the end of the war, and then split by the Berlin Wall.

The first place Jack took me was to the Rhine, the wide and busy waterway that bisected the city. There we parked on a bench in the sunshine, watching impossibly long barges float up and down the river, while little white ferryboats wove among them. It was like watching an orderly parade of vehicles with the sound turned off. Despite my fatigue from the long trip, I felt both mind and body begin to relax and a willingness to let the city work its magic on me. Jack had already fallen in love with Bonn, despite the circumstances of our visit. He had decided to put his trust in this new approach to his treatment, and he was determined to enjoy the process as much as he could.

"Hallo, are you English or American?" A small, clean-shaven man sitting next to us asked. We would hear this question often.

"American," we said, smiling and trying to look humble in the early days of Reagan's presidency.

He gazed out over the river and after a while said, "I was there when I was sixteen. I liked it very much."

"That's nice," I replied. "Where did you go?"

"Montana, Idaho, Utah. I was a prisoner of war."

"Oh." I caught my breath, even though this didn't feel like a confrontation.

"I was very lucky." After a silence he continued. "I was captured only four days after I went to the front. The Americans always treated me well. They gave me cigarettes. At first, I wasn't allowed to work, but after a while they looked the other way, and I was able to pick apples and peaches. I even earned some money. If I hadn't been captured…." He made a guttural sound and drew his index finger across his neck. "Yes, I was very lucky."

Lucky indeed, considering what happened to most of his compatriots!

During our months in Bonn, we spent many hours exploring the city. For most of his treatment, Jack felt well enough to go out, and we developed a routine that was not unlike that of tourists, but with certain responsibilities like chemotherapy and radiation during weekdays.

Along with several of our American friends also being treated in the Janker Klinik, we grew to love Bonn as a home away from home. It was as if the liveliness of the "Bonner Sommer," as it was called, was infectious.

The streets of Bonn teemed with bicycles, and the sidewalks were full of cafes packed with students. The city center consisted of a whole mile of pedestrian way. Three separate squares were surrounded by shops and cafes, and apartments were perched above the shops so the city never lost its feeling of aliveness, even after the shops and restaurants closed, unlike so many downtowns in U.S. cities that died after about 6:00 p.m.

The square closest to our hotel was the Post Platz, where, not surprisingly, the post office resided, and also the cathedral, or Münster, which looked to me like an overgrown village church. Just down the street from the Post Platz was Beethoven's birthplace, a typical Bonner townhouse painted a soft yellow with boxes of geraniums stationed along the wrought-iron fence. A statue of the great maestro dominated the Post Platz, shoulders hunched, forehead furrowed above the bushy eyebrows. It was Beethoven, not the capital buildings that the city had always proudly claimed as its own.

Most evenings, we would walk downtown after dinner. There we encountered a big, extended village, alive with music, food, wine, and talk. Students in doorways played Bach on flute and violin, while passers-by dropped coins into their instrument cases. People drank coffee and wine in dozens of cafes that sprang up on the pavement whenever the weather allowed. Everyone—young people, prosperous burghers and their solid wives, children, old folks—all strolled through the squares arm-in-arm, window-shopping, which we learned was a great German pastime. Sometimes, the sound of the shawm and viola d'amore would float out from a Renaissance consort in the central square. Other times, mimes or dancers would perform. During the day, a one-man band would stroll through the Post Platz, beating drums and cymbals, and playing a harmonica all at the same time. I had never seen a place that was so vibrant and yet so civilized.

When we passed strangers on our strolls, I learned to nod and say, *"Guten Tag"* or *"Guten Abend."* The locals accepted those of us from the Janker Klinik without stares or comments, even though some patients were bald, some walked with canes, and others were pushed in wheelchairs. A surprising number of us were Americans.

Jack and I had always made a point to visit the local art museum wherever we travelled, and we found that Bonn's Kunstmuseum housed a superb collection of Rhenish Expressionists. This is where we discovered another one of Bonn's famous sons, August Macke, an early 20th century painter who was killed during World War I when he was only twenty-seven years old. His work displayed the flat perspective and intense colors of the Fauvists and his mentor, Henri Matisse, and later, the brilliant, luminous colors of Der Blaue Reiter school and his friends Franz Marc and Wassily Kandinsky. We fell in love with Macke and bought a poster of the *Rotes Haus im Park,* which we hung in every one of our homes in our later life. Just to look at its dazzling pinks, greens, and golds reminded us of our summer in this unexpectedly magical German town.

CHAPTER EIGHT
The Janker Klinik

After Jack was admitted to the clinic as an inpatient, I moved to an even smaller room in the cowboy hotel. This began a period of loneliness, but fortunately I had brought my flute along and enjoyed playing while looking out my tiny window at the angular rooftops and flowered courtyards of neighboring houses. The fact that I was interrupting the austerity of German afternoons vaguely appealed to my usually well-controlled rebellious nature. After a couple of weeks, I moved to the Kurfürstenhof, a more amiable hotel with a livelier breakfast scene and a larger room.

The treatment regimen at the Janker Klinik was somewhat surprising to both of us. Although we really had no idea what the protocol would be, we expected something "alternative," like large doses of vitamins and enzymes. Instead, Jack was scheduled for radiation treatments and chemotherapy with chemicals that were not yet available in the U.S. The radiation machine was alarmingly low-tech, and we worried that in the process of zapping his tumor, the radiation would damage nearby tissues. In fact, Jack lost several teeth due to radiation spillover, but nothing more critical seemed to have been damaged.

The clinic's one innovation was the addition of ultrasound to his protocol, which they described as "Warm Therapy." When I would stop by Jack's room and ask his neighbor, *"Wo ist Jack?"* he would reply with something that sounded like *"varm terap."* Nobody minded the ultrasound therapy because it felt good. Jack would often go to sleep, as he did when I was giving him bodywork like acupressure or foot massages.

Although this was not exactly the treatment we expected, we decided to go along with whatever Dr. Scheef, the chief physician, recommended. All the doctors were kind and solicitous, as were the nurses, and Jack especially liked the young Dr. Lange, who sported a perfect tan, a condition that Jack had always admired and sought to emulate.

As far as I could tell, the treatment at the *Janker Klinik* was not all that different from what Jack would have received at an American clinic, except for the difference in chemicals, and the addition of ultrasound therapy. The clinic itself, at least at that time, lacked the glossy decor of an American hospital in favor of simple functionality, and the equipment was not as modern. However, Dr. Scheef claimed the chemicals were more advanced than those used in the U.S.

Unlike many of the clinic's patients, Jack was feeling quite well when he arrived, and the treatment rarely bothered him significantly. He was well enough to wander around town, and eventually decided that the food, ambience, and company were better in my hotel, so he moved in with me. He went to the clinic regularly for his treatments, and he kept his bed there just in case. The only time Jack was restricted from going anywhere was when his white blood count fell literally to zero and he was in serious danger of becoming infected with whatever was going around. The rest of the time he behaved unofficially as an outpatient, something he would not likely have been allowed to do in the U.S. He was convinced they referred to him as the "disappearing American," but in the tradition of the clinic, nobody wanted to interfere with a patient's happiness. Jack wanted to be with his wife, stroll around, and enjoy Bonn's festive scene. We were both happy with that arrangement, and I no longer felt so alone.

The Janker Klinik had developed an international reputation, especially among Americans, due mainly to the enthusiasm of a popular American journalist, Patrick McGrady, who had been highly critical of the American cancer establishment. Until his death in 2003, McGrady provided consulting services to cancer patients who wanted information on alternative and complementary treatments. He had interviewed Dr. Scheef and spread the word about the clinic's success with treatments not available in the U.S.

Consequently, there were two other American couples in residence with whom we became fast friends and formed a sort of expatriate club. We first met Rocky and Fanny in the city center while listening to a concert. Rocky was tall, handsome, and broad-shouldered with a long mane of gray hair. He was pushing a wheelchair with a pale but pretty, turbaned woman. We were convinced Rocky was a rock star, but found out subsequently that he was a Western artist who had worked for a time as a lumberjack. (Later in his life, Rocky would become a successful artist with paintings in galleries and collections nationwide.) Fanny was also an artist and an imaginative homemaker, and they lived on a small farm outside Seattle. Fanny made practically everything the family used—she spun, wove, sewed, and made things from animal skins. She dressed her two little girls, Cody and Cheyenne (at that time with relatives back home), as well as herself in her homemade products. Only about five feet tall, she was a little dynamo, now laid low by ovarian cancer.

The other couple we quickly grew to love was John and Alvin from Los Angeles. Alvin was a mild-mannered architect who had studied with Frank Lloyd Wright and had developed a successful practice in Hollywood. John had been a hotshot graphic artist with a major advertising firm in Los Angeles. He had eventually decided to leave a world that had grown distasteful to him and struck out as a fine artist on his own. Upon first meeting Alvin, John told us, "I said to myself, *This man is glorious! Sensational!*" I felt similarly about both of them.

Two years earlier, John had developed rectal cancer, but his treatment had not been successful. By the time he and Alvin came to Bonn, John was so weak he could barely walk. However, he seemed to perk up after a couple of weeks of treatment at the Janker Klinik.

Because of the clinic's loose visiting hours, we were often able to hang out with these friends. Whenever John and Fanny were strong enough, we would all go out on the town. This happened more frequently with John than with Fanny, but on one occasion all six of us did go out to dinner. At other times, we would gather either in John's or Fanny's room in the clinic, telling jokes, sharing information about cancer treatments, and gossiping about the clinic personnel. We all wondered where *did* Dr. Lange get his beautiful tan. John seemed to know all about the clinic staff, the fact that Dr. Scheef drove a Mercedes coupe, and that all the nurses were to be called *"Schwester"* even though they weren't nuns. More than once we were told by one of the nurses to keep the decibel level down.

Since I had become a foot reflexology enthusiast, sometimes I would try my new healing art on John or Fanny. But I found out quickly that not everybody was as strong as Jack, who, not only being much healthier than either of them, was also a newly discovered bodywork sponge. He just drank in any kind of hands-on treatment. But John and Fanny were so sensitive (and so ill), they could barely tolerate even a gentle foot massage. After Fanny's first try, she couldn't tolerate it at all. Her feet were so tiny, like those of a child. It almost broke my heart.

Fanny and Rocky returned home to Seattle about three weeks after we first arrived. John and Alvin left for L.A. about three weeks later. We later learned that Fanny died a few months after returning home, and John survived for almost a year. Fortunately, I was able to visit John and Alvin in L.A. a few months before John died. We corresponded with Rocky for the first few years, then lost touch, but I have seen his vibrant paintings on the internet. Years later, I am still in occasional contact with Alvin, whom I consider one of my all-time favorite people.

Interestingly, both John and Alvin, as well as Jack, have said that those months in Bonn were some of the happiest of their lives. I might even say the same for myself, and I have often wondered how much that sort of happiness and friendship can contribute to healing.

CHAPTER NINE
Forays into
New Kinds of Healing

Thanks to advice from Alvin, Jack and I moved into an even nicer small hotel near the clinic called the Esplanade, where we ended up staying for the better part of three months. Ben and Jana Urbach, a Czech Jewish couple who had moved to Bonn in the 1960s, ran the Esplanade. Ben had been a chef in London and later in Berlin. Exactly why they moved to Germany I was never quite sure, because they bemoaned the fact that there were so few Jews left in Germany, and they felt it was difficult to make friends. In fact, they had to import a rabbi from Strasbourg to perform the *bris* on their infant son.

Breakfast at the Esplanade was a far cry from the hushed atmosphere of "the morgue," our nickname for the breakfast room of our first hotel. Now, there was jaunty pop music on the radio (which we surreptitiously turned down), and pot after pot of rich black coffee.

During our three-month stay, I drank so much of it that I developed tinnitus (ringing in my ears) and had to stop coffee, even decaf, after returning home. Although Ben didn't cook for most of his guests, he must have known we were kindred souls, so he offered to fix dinners for us. Besides, most of the Esplanade patrons were only there for a few days, whereas we virtually lived there. Ben cooked us a variety of German dishes, including Wiener Schnitzel, Sauerbraten, and roast pork with vegetables. Sometime during the meal, Ben would come out and ask us how it was, and he would stand there, wringing his hands, until we gave him the feedback he wanted. In truth, his meals were nourishing but rather bland, and it wasn't beyond us to sneak in a jar of garlic salt, which I kept in my purse and sprinkled on the main course when he wasn't looking. In spite of, or perhaps even because of the uninspiring food, Ben's cooking was reminiscent of my mother's, and I felt exceptionally well taken care of.

Throughout our stay in Germany, except for the periods when Jack was restricted to the clinic, I gave him acupressure every day. The routine Bonnie had given me was to benefit the upper thorax and respiratory system. Jack would lie on his back on the bed, and I would kneel on the floor next to him with Bonnie's chart propped up against his abdomen. I started with my right hand on his right upper arm and my left hand on his right palm, pressing my fingers into the appropriate spot. After about a minute, I would move to the next position, which was my left hand to the inside of his rib cage slightly to the right. The next position after that was my right hand to the top of his pubic bone and my left hand to the top of his left thigh. I continued this routine to various spots on his back and legs, and then reversed the whole process.

For the first few weeks, I depended on the chart, but soon I had the whole routine memorized. It was amazingly easy to find the appropriate acupressure spot because Jack always knew when I had hit it. I would move my fingers in the vicinity of the spot on Bonnie's map, and Jack would say, "No, not yet, no," and then, "That's it!" The signal was that he felt a slight sensitivity, a little twinge. He had felt that same twinge in every spot that Bonnie had touched when she treated him in Maryland. I had no such sign to guide me, although sometimes I did feel a little buzzing sensation in my fingers after I had stayed in the same spot for a minute or so.

After I was adept at finding the right acupressure spot, Jack could fall asleep, which he did every time. The whole process was peaceful and refreshing for both of us, no matter what was going on during his treatment or whatever kind of relationship stress we were under—and there was plenty of that kind of stress as we plowed deeper into the psychotherapeutic process once we had returned home.

In Germany, Jack and I had sought out what we thought would be alternative medicine, although the "alternatives" provided by the Janker Klinik were more conventional than what we had anticipated. But through the influence of Dr. Schildwaechter in Washington, and Barbara, our therapist, we had started to open up to ideas that were quite different from our usual perspectives. Acupressure instruction from Bonnie was our first foray into a way of thinking that had been accepted for thousands of years by Asian civilizations, but was still considered "radical" in the West. The idea that healing in one part of the body could be facilitated by pressing remote spots in other parts, well, we probably would have considered ridiculous a few years earlier. But now, both of us were open to almost anything, and in the subsequent months, we tried almost anything.

We had brought two books along to Germany that had a major influence on our thinking. Dr. Schildwaechter had recommended one called *Joy's Way: A Map for the Transformational Journey* by the physician–turned–radical healer, W. Brugh Joy, M.D. The author had been a successful young physician in Los Angeles who had discovered that he could tell much about a person's state of health just by running his hands an inch or so above the person's body. He had unwittingly discovered the chakras, energy centers that were well known to Eastern practitioners for thousands of years, but either unknown or considered mysterious to most people in the West.

Thus, Dr. Joy stumbled onto what we now call energy medicine. In his words: "…the supposedly solid human body turns out to be an intricate interweaving of energy fields; where disease is not an entity but rather a fixated warp of energy interactions...."

He also made statements like this: "...Unconditional Love transcends the limitations of personal love; where mortality itself dies—and becomes immortality..."

Although we didn't really understand a lot of it, Jack and I were fascinated by this heady stuff. Since we were reading it in an environment far from home, we were much more willing to let go of our more linear and concrete modes of thinking. Exciting ideas like these gave additional validation to the journey we had already begun to embrace. So, we accepted without reservation the benefits to be gained from acupressure and reflexology, and we were open to all the seemingly bizarre events that occurred later along the way. In time, we came to believe there were too many transformative events to be merely coincidence and, therefore, must have been instances of grace.

The other book that had a significant influence on our thinking was *Getting Well Again* by O. Carl Simonton, M.D., Stephanie Matthews Simonton, and James Creighton, Ph.D. Actually, my sister-in-law, Ann, had sent it to us when Jack was first diagnosed in 1982, but we were so steeped in the culture of conventional medicine that we paid no attention to it. In fact, I had taken a look at the table of contents, saw a chapter on "the mind-body connection" and another on "personality, stress, and cancer," and said to myself, "No thanks." At the time, Jack didn't even glance at it.

Now that conventional medicine had failed us, however, we were receptive to what the Simontons had to offer. The first half of the book made an excellent case for the link between stress and illness. The Simontons went so far as to suggest that there was a "cancer personality" in which well-socialized, nice people tolerated frustration for years, allowing unexpressed anger and resentment literally to eat away at the physical body. On reading this, I was offended and felt like it was a blame-the-victim approach. Jack, on the other hand, accepted it completely. "Yep, that's me. Pissed off at the old man [he had never called him Dad], pissed off at Ronald Reagan, and pissed off at all these pussycat Democrats who won't stand up for their own programs."

I could have added pissed off at his ignorant and spiteful stepmother, at his disingenuous boss, and at all the people who drove too slowly in the left lane. But he never really expressed it—he just swallowed it, and drank.

Despite the beer machine in the Janker Klinik, Jack didn't drink much in Bonn, and he had plenty of time to read and think and practice the exercises the Simontons recommended. The second half of *Getting Well Again* described pathways to health: how to participate in your own cure, how to overcome resentment, and some practical methods of relaxation and visual imagery. This book was our introduction to the art of visualization, a practice that we both continued over the next twenty years.

As recommended by the Simontons, Jack started with the visualization specific to his cancer. He did the whole-body relaxation exercise followed by a mental picture of his tumor surrounded by white light. At first he imagined a little Pac-Man character gobbling up his tumor, but after a while, he shifted to an image he liked better. He visualized the tumor as a dirty sponge, and he visualized his treatment as crows pecking away at it and finally consuming it.

In later editions of the book, the Simontons recommended visualizing one's own white blood cells doing the work—armies of them winning the battle with ease and carrying away the dead cancer cells. Then the dead cells were eliminated in urine and stool. This was the expectation of what would happen, and with it would come energy, appetite, and a feeling of being loved.

Jack performed this ritual faithfully, twice a day, and I often joined him. Much later, we read about the scientific confirmation of this kind of process, but at the time we visualized because it seemed like the right thing to do.

CHAPTER TEN
Showdown at the Post Office

Fortunately, my clients were flexible about deadlines, and I was able to continue my consulting work at my own pace. One of my projects was to prepare myself as an expert witness in a case where railroad workers were suing Conrail for damage to their hearing. At one point, I needed to call the lawyer I was working with, but I didn't know how to use the telephones, and my German was practically nonexistent. I had studied German for a few months in the seventh grade, and I knew how to say, *"Fröhliche Weihnachten und ein glükliches neues Jahr."* (Merry Christmas and Happy New Year), and a few more practical phrases, like *bitte, danke,* and *"Sprechen Sie Englisch?"* but that was the extent of it.

Then, our paternal innkeeper told me that the cheapest way to telephone was at the post office. So, I walked downtown to the big yellow baroque building and stood in line. When my turn finally came, I smiled at the impassive bureaucrat behind the counter and said, *"Sprechen Sie Englisch?"* in my best accent.

"Nein."

"Bitte, I need to make a telephone call," I said, gesturing with my thumb at my ear and my little finger toward my mouth.

He then uttered a stream of German that didn't sound very friendly.

"Ich verstehe nicht," I stammered.

After the same stream of unfriendliness, he pointed to a telephone booth across the room. I stood helpless because I didn't know what I was supposed to do when I got there. The bureaucrat then turned to the man behind me, acting as though I had become invisible. No one offered any help. All the attractions of Bonn suddenly vanished, and I became a foreigner in an inhospitable land with a sick husband and no friends. As I walked through the door, I held my head high even though my vision had already begun to blur. Outside, I cried for a while, and then I knew what I had to do.

The first place I tried was Berlitz. They could guarantee that I would be conversant in German within two weeks, but the price was astronomical. So I decided that I needed a tutor, perhaps a graduate student. The next place was a bookstore on the way back to the hotel. This time my *Sprechen Sie English* was greeted politely, and the sales clerk found an attractive young woman to advise me. After she wrote a name and phone number on a scrap of paper, I went right back to the hotel and made the phone call. The name of my tutor was Anke Schomaker-Huett, the sister of the helpful bookstore clerk and a graduate student in education. We made an appointment for 4:00 the next afternoon. Little did I know that this was the beginning of one of the most important friendships of my life.

Anke's apartment was in a large house about a mile up the hill from our hotel. Every other day for several weeks I took the bus up the hill, and Anke welcomed me into her quiet and comfortable home. She always had tea and cookies waiting, and she rested the teapot on a heavy glass holder with six vertical pillars surrounding a tea-light candle. The flickering candle, reflected in that lovely sculpture, seemed to mirror the radiance of Anke's spirit.

Although I learned a good deal of German, my memories of that relationship are more focused on Anke. She was the modern German equivalent of a Botticelli beauty with her clear blue eyes and halo of curly blonde hair. Before every lesson, we spent at least fifteen minutes speaking English so I could tell her how Jack was doing and how I was feeling. I held nothing back and would cry at times, while she listened sympathetically.

Once in the middle of the lesson, a little bird came into the living room through the French doors and hopped around on the carpet. When I gasped and pointed, she just smiled and said, "Oh yes, he likes to visit often." Another time in the middle of my halting recitation, she jumped up and exclaimed, "Dat flower!" With apologies she filled a pitcher and watered a drooping houseplant.

Only months before our arrival in Germany, my mother had died and my husband had received a dire prognosis, and now, I was flailing away at managing our lives in a country where I didn't speak the language. This young woman was quietly providing the kindness that I so desperately needed. One day, when I was browsing in a bookstore, I stumbled across, of all things, a book called *Joy's Weg*. It was my new favorite book, *Joy's Way*, translated into German. I snatched it up and presented it to Anke at our next lesson. She was pleased, as she and her husband, Udo, were both quite interested in the body-mind connection and matters of the spirit. "It is not chance," she told me, "that you and I were brought together."

I knew she was right.

After a few weeks, Anke announced that she needed to start commuting to Dusseldorf, where she had to perform a period of practice teaching, so she could not continue our lessons. Before I panicked, however, she said that Udo had agreed to continue the lessons. My heart sank, but I had met Udo, and though he could never take her place, I liked him and wanted to continue becoming self-sufficient in German. Udo was completing a doctoral degree in philosophy at the University of Bonn. Tall, thin, and intense, he was a more rigorous teacher than Anke, but tolerant of my mistakes and incomplete homework assignments.

By the time we left Bonn, I was able to compose a simple autobiography in German, *"Ich bin im Jahr 1937 in Illinois geboren. Mein Vater war ein Architekt..."* etc. I could also buy things in stores and order a meal in a restaurant. I even made a triumphant appearance at the post office where I successfully bought the appropriate stamps, although I never again had to use the telephone. Better yet, I actually had a simple conversation in German with a lovely young man one day on the train to Cologne.

Anke and Udo became our good friends while we were in Bonn, and we went out to dinner together a couple of times. Udo told us how he met Anke. He was at a party and saw this golden-haired beauty on the other side of the room. He made up his mind before he even met her that he would marry her. "I knew she was an angel," he said.

I knew he was right.

CHAPTER ELEVEN
The Tough Love Approach

After the first six weeks of treatment, Jack's CT scans showed considerable improvement. The tumor had shrunk to about one quarter of its original size, so the doctors gave us a two-week respite, and we decided to go home.

We loved the European train system where the trains ran on the minute. The clock on the platform in Bonn even had a second hand. Each coach was identified with its destination, in our case Brussels via Cologne and Aachen. In Brussels, we changed trains for Oostende, then onto the hydrofoil and across the Channel, where after only about two hours the chalky cliffs of Dover rose into view. Onward to London on a rail system that, having been privatized by Margaret Thatcher, was like an impoverished relative in comparison to its European cousins. We were rested and traveling in daylight for the return trip, so we were much more inclined to enjoy the adventure.

After a night in a London hotel, we were back on British Air and finally home to our comfortable house, kids, friends, and our ecstatic dog, Max. Then began the tough work.

Our therapist, Barbara, was ready for us, and Jack had made an appointment with her the next afternoon. At the end of the hour session, she told Jack that she wanted to see me as well. When he brought that message home, I told him, "I've really had enough therapy, thanks, and I'm doing okay."

Somehow, I knew she meant business, and I wasn't eager to get sucked in. However, Barbara called to make sure that I was coming, so I dutifully complied.

Barbara held her therapy sessions in her house, mostly in the kitchen. She felt no need for a formal office and much preferred the cozy setting of her home. Her house had its own characteristic musky scent, like patchouli, and the decor was New Age comfortable with pictures of Indian gurus and saints throughout. She always offered us herbal tea and sometimes treats like cookies, dates, nuts, or raw bean sprouts. We would meet in the kitchen, outdoors in the backyard, or up on the third floor, depending on what kind of work needed to be done. The third floor was for the more active processes and where the groups met. She had recommended that we join her couples' group in addition to our individual sessions.

Barbara's approach was to see each of us separately for a few minutes, then work with us as a couple. Not being a stickler for time, she would sometimes spend more than an hour with us together, especially if there were difficult issues that needed resolution on the spot. At times, we would walk out past other clients who had been waiting for half an hour, and other times, it was we who did the waiting while other clients worked through their emergencies.

In fact, Barbara was an example of a brilliant, intuitive therapist whose unconventional methods could bring dramatic improvements, as they did with us, while her attention to practical details, such as her billing methods, could be a source of frustration. But what she lacked in left-brained organization, she more than made up in skill and imagination, always working from and with the heart.

In my first session with Barbara, she drew everything out, including the buried grief about my mother's death, my anger about Jack's continuing involvement with Margot, my disappointment at how poorly we communicated, and the whole panoply of emotions surrounding Jack's cancer: fear of abandonment, desperate concern for this person whom I had grown to love more deeply, and frustration at not being able to control nearly any aspect of my life. She also brought out the terrible conflicts I felt about my affair, which I had waited to reveal until the end of that first session.

When I was finished, she said, "You'll have to tell him."

I was horrified. "No, I can't do that."

"Yes you can. You must tell him."

"No, it wouldn't do any good at all and just upset him."
I was falling back on the excuse that one mustn't upset the
cancer patient.

"We're going to have no secrets in here," declared
Barbara. "If he's going to get well, he has to know the
truth. You complained about how the two of you weren't
communicating. Now, you're going to communicate."

This wasn't the only time I wanted to race out of
Barbara's house and away from her iron hand. But
moments later when we started our session together,
Barbara said in her sweet, Southern-belle voice, "Alice has
something she wants to tell you." And so I told him.

Jack was indeed upset and hurt, not so much for the
fact of my infidelity, but because I had desired another
man and had acted on that. He felt injured and dimin-
ished, and it took us the better part of two years to work
through the pain and bitterness on both sides. I vowed
to myself never to betray him again, and it was a very
easy promise to keep.

Barbara's sessions, while not what I would call enjoy-
able, were always useful. They enabled us to face and
eventually accept many of the emotions embedded in
our relationship that we felt were socially unacceptable.
She encouraged me to acknowledge my anger at Jack
for having cancer. While I was committed to being his
partner in all of this, caring for him and being at his
side—at the same time, I was furious at him for being
so needy. Who is going to make sure that he takes his

pills, calls the doctor, and remembers his appointments if I don't do it? Who is going to pay all the bills? Who is going to make sure he eats right? And then, isn't one always supposed to be gentle and compassionate with someone who has cancer?

From the beginning, Jack and I had been independent people. I had never been married before and had learned to take care of myself as a matter of course. Jack had done much of the cooking in his previous marriage, and Margot had done the childcare, but he hadn't relied on her for support. In our relationship, neither Jack nor I had spent much time or energy taking care of each other, so this kind of responsibility was new for me. Although I jumped to fulfill what I saw as a need, there was a part of me that also resented it.

Barbara called it "the tyranny of the sick." Jack wasn't weak and frail the way cancer patients often are, but in his own way, he really did want to be taken care of. It was something he hadn't had for a long time.

At times in therapy Barbara would have one of us hold a big, firm pillow while she made the other one hit the pillow with a battacca, a padded bat, and scream whatever came to mind. We were both reluctant hitters, socialized to be "nice" people, and afraid to let loose the storm of contained anger.

Since Jack was often hesitant to start yelling, she would prompt him. "Bitch, take care of me!" she would make him say. Then on the pillow: Whap! Pow! "I hate you for cheating on me! I hate you for never giving me enough attention!"

When it was my turn to hit, Barbara would start me off with, "You bastard, how dare you get cancer! How dare you check out on me!" More pounding, then I would pause, breathless, and she would say, "Go on, Alice."

"I hate you for being sick! I hate you for spending all my money!"

After those kinds of sessions we would drive home silently, getting through the week as best we could, not relishing the idea of the next session.

Barbara was not about to let us waste any time by bullshitting her or ourselves. More than once she told us that we had no time to screw around. These were literally life-and-death matters. Sometimes, the intensity of the therapeutic process felt like more than I could bear. Once, after one of our group sessions, I felt so overwhelmed I refused to go back to the group. Barbara didn't accept this and she had one member of the group call and plead with me. I sat listening to Jill's voice on the answering machine, and finally, having steeled myself for another painful session, got in my car and drove over to Barbara's house. Looking back on those times, I realize that Barbara must have known that we could take her tough love approach or else she wouldn't have pushed us so hard. Besides, she made sure that at the end of every session, she brought us to a place of love. It was as if she made us dig until we reached the vast reservoir of good will that lay beneath the bitter landscape of all our conflicts.

Our two-week interlude flew by, and the next thing we knew, we were back on British Air headed for London, Dover, Oostende, Cologne, and Bonn for another four weeks of chemotherapy, radiation, German lessons, and the festivities of a "Bonner Sommer." This time, however, we weren't enjoying ourselves quite so much because the angst of the therapeutic process was very much with us. We often found ourselves quarreling over the customary issues of money and sex. In addition to his resentment of my infidelity, I was angry that Jack was paying generous alimony to Margot when he couldn't afford to pay for his own treatment. Fortunately, the fees at the Janker Klinik were ridiculously low by American standards, and my mother's legacy, along with my consulting practice, paid for our hotel and multiple trips across the Atlantic.

CHAPTER TWELVE
A European Respite

As the weeks wore on, Jack continued to make good progress with his treatment. A CT scan toward the end of the second four weeks showed his tumor to be greatly reduced. There were times when the chemotherapy caused him to feel depleted, and he didn't have the energy to walk around town, so I would go out and buy food, and we would picnic in our room.

There was a lovely little store not far from the hotel where I could buy a variety of cheeses. Even though they looked distinctly different from each other, to Jack they all tasted like Brie. The chemo didn't seem to have affected his appetite, even for rich food like cheese, but Jack wanted something stronger. So he commissioned me to get some Danish blue, which I brought back the next day. To him it was Brie with a few bluish specks in it. After that, I asked for a gamey looking hunk labeled Gorgonzola. Again, to Jack it was Brie, only thinly disguised. What would have been a luxury in the U.S. suddenly became an annoyance, but he ate it anyway.

Most of the time, however, Jack felt good enough to respond to the lure of downtown Bonn where we sipped coffee at sidewalk cafés, window-shopped, listened to the street musicians, and allowed ourselves to be jostled by German matrons seriously shopping in the Galeria Kaufhof department store. We often ate lunch downtown, and Jack would marvel at the old grannies who socked away a whole plate of knuckle or wurst, sauerkraut, and spaetzle. "Look at them," he would say, "and they're not even fat!"

During the afternoon, Jack would nap while I went up the hill for my German lesson, after which we would plan our evening. It was as if we were in some kind of dream in which cancer played only a minor role.

At the end of the second four weeks of treatment, the clinic gave us another two-week respite. This time, instead of going home, we decided to stay in Europe. It happened that my father was visiting his English cousins in London, so we joined him for a few days. Although we stayed in a more modest hotel, we saw him regularly and had the traditional Sunday lunch with various cousins (first, second, and once or twice removed). It was wonderful being around all my relatives and especially my loving and supportive father. However, I didn't want to tell him about the additional strain caused by the marital problems that had begun to unfold during our work with Barbara.

Experiencing such intense and revealing therapy, and then leaving the country for several weeks was tough without the benefit of our therapist to guide us when we got stuck. There were occasions when Jack and I would degenerate into anger and blame, and the temptation would be to erect a wall between us. But Barbara had instructed us to maintain intimacy, physical as well as emotional, no matter what, and we always tried to access the place of mutual respect and affection no matter how deeply it would seem to be buried. The pathway to intimacy could be confession, joint meditation, tears, or sex, but the goal was always to move through the block to the other side.

Although we were often able to do this in Bonn, somehow we were not so successful in London where I desperately tried to put up a good front for my father. The results seemed to be even nastier exchanges between Jack and me, full of blame, dissatisfaction with our sex life, and whatever else we could think of, while I pretended to my father that everything was fine. The dubious policy of "protecting" others by not revealing the truth had always run strong in my family, and I was still learning that it was a bad idea.

After a few days, we decided to go to France and bought a Nicholson's Guide to Normandy and Brittany. We set off by train to Southampton, then by ferry to Dieppe, and again by train to Rouen, landing in the famous Art Nouveau train station with its one-side-only clock tower. We found a hotel near the station, and after a restless night in a lumpy bed, set off in a rental car. We had hardly gone beyond the city limits of Rouen when the window on the driver's side of the little Renault fell down into the door and refused to be cranked up, so we took the car back and started off again in another little Renault. Because we thought Jack knew everything there was to know about cars, we didn't think to consult the manual, and as it turned out, there wasn't one.

Our first stop was the picturesque harbor town of Honfleur, once home of the École de Honfleur, a focal point of Impressionism first developed in Paris in the 1860s. Artists like Claude Monet and the composer Erik Satie had lived in Honfleur, inspired by its beauty. We stopped to photograph the Hotel Cheval Blanc so we could send a picture to our art-loving friend, Frank Schaefer, who owned an inn of the same name (White Horse Inn) in Provincetown. We could see why this floating world of brightly colored buildings and sparkling sea provided inspiration to the Impressionists. It was as if we had journeyed away from German tidiness and English stiff upper lip to the sensuality of France.

It was evening when we stopped in Bayeux, the Norman town famed for its historic tapestry. We found a lovely inexpensive hotel, feasted on boef bourguignon, braised leeks, tiny potatoes, and of course, plenty of the local red wine. This dinner was more delicious than anything we had eaten in Bonn. Satisfied, we fell into a sound sleep in a luxurious bed. It was practically noon when we awakened and gazed into a sun-drenched courtyard overflowing with brilliant red geraniums. Making love that morning was easy and precious, enveloped by flowered sheets, a red satin duvet, and a pervasive French ambience. Worry and resentment seemed to melt into the past and were no longer a part of our baggage. It was as if we were participating in some miraculous French cure, transformed into traveling companions on a new voyage, living only in the moment, open to every surprise, every new sensation.

This languorous approach to life and travel held for the entire trip through Normandy and Brittany, and we ended up driving all of about thirty kilometers per day. Our route took us to Mont Saint Michel where we climbed to the top and watched a few brave tourists meandering about the muddy flats far below. I remembered how my father, who had lived in France for a while, told me that the tide here came in as fast as a horse could gallop. After our climb, we ate omelettes at Mère Poulard's, just as my parents and I had done thirty years earlier when they had taken my brother and me to France as a graduation present. I had forgotten how exquisitely frothy these omelets were—more like a soufflé, but still delicious.

At Avranches, we were the lone picnickers in the beautiful Jardin des Plantes and slept that night on a horsehair mattress in a high bed, big enough to hold an entire family. It felt like going back to an earlier century. The next day, after observing an older gentleman eating seafood over shaved ice from a three-tiered, glass and wire apparatus, we ordered the same thing, along with the mildly alcoholic sparkling cider of the region. While we feasted, we were entertained watching the interplay between the older man and his mini-skirted mistress, at least thirty years his junior. It reminded me of other people-watching episodes we had shared on earlier trips to Italy and Greece in the carefree days before our marriage. Now, it seemed like we were having the honeymoon that we hadn't allowed ourselves after our wedding, at the time too busy with work and responsibilities.

In the afternoon, we visited Patton Square in Avranches, complete with a Sherman tank, honoring General Patton's liberation of the city from the Germans during WW II. To this day, Americans are much appreciated here.

Then, onward to Brittany and Saint Malo, where we found a hotel on the beach, and drove into the walled town for a late dinner. After dinner, we ended up driving the several miles back to our hotel in the dark because, after much fumbling and cursing, neither of us was able to find the switch to turn on the headlights—and, of course, there was no manual. The irony of being killed by a French eighteen-wheeler because we couldn't find the damned light switch, after having survived so much and so long, didn't really occur to us because the situation, however maddening, seemed funny, especially after another delicious meal with plenty of good red wine.

We continued our way through Brittany, stopping at the 16th-century Renaissance castle Château de la Motte Glain and then to the medieval castle at Vitré, both of which impressed us with their massive stone towers capped by conical roofs. Finally, we arrived in Rennes where we turned in the car. That night we had a last gorge of French cuisine: *pâté de foie gras, escalope de veau,* salad, two kinds of wine, cheese, and a generous dollop of chocolate mousse. Jack was able to withstand this onslaught despite the warnings of the NIH medical staff, who had advised him to eat only light meals four or five times a day. But somehow, he was able to moderate. Not I. By the time we boarded the train for Paris, I had eaten so much rich food I was nauseous, expecting to have to run to the bathroom at any moment. Jack credited my salvation to a little boy in the seat in front of us with whom I played peek-a-boo for most of the trip.

In Paris, we changed trains for Cologne, and then on to Bonn, back to the Hotel Esplanade, the Janker Klinik, and for Jack, back to chemotherapy and radiation. Honeymoon over.

CHAPTER THIRTEEN
No Secrets

I continued my German lessons with Udo because Anke had started her practice teaching in Düsseldorf. Jack had taken six years of German and could read and write it with some degree of accomplishment, although he would always push me in front when it was necessary to speak.

One day while we sat in a restaurant waiting for our meal, I was working on my assignment from Udo. When I asked Jack a question he couldn't answer, another customer sitting nearby provided it. We began to converse in English, and the gentleman asked if we were in Bonn on business or holiday. Jack replied that we were attending the Janker Klinik. The man was amazed that Jack was not a doctor but a patient. He then proceeded to tell us about a formula for cancer that the old Russians used with some success after doctors had pronounced them hopeless: Take a large ripe aloe vera leaf and put it in a blender with $1/2$ cup of port wine and $1/2$ cup of honey. If the mixture is not quite liquid enough add a little water, then drink it.

When we got home, Jack told the story to his brother, Bob, in Texas. Bob immediately sent a friend into the desert to collect aloe vera leaves, and promptly sent a carton of them to us by UPS. Jack whipped up a concoction in a blender and drank two tablespoons twice a day for about a month. He said it was delicious.

Treatment at the Janker Klinik progressed as before with chemotherapy, radiation, and ultrasound, and I went up the hill every other day for German lessons with Udo. Jack was feeling well enough to stay with me in the hotel full time, and the painful spats we had experienced before our trip to France had abated. We continued our evening strolls downtown for dinner or coffee in the sidewalk cafés, window-shopping, and enjoying the festive Bonner Sommer nights.

Toward the end of our fourth month, the doctors gave Jack another CT scan. Before we received the results officially, one of the doctors saw me walking in the hall and called me into his office, which had never occurred before. With no preliminaries, he launched into his spiel.

"The tumor is growing back fast. It is now completely surrounding the stomach. It looks very bad, but don't tell your husband."

I was floored. Just six weeks earlier the tumor had been cooperatively shrinking. Up until now, everything had seemed to be onward and upward, and this sort of prognosis was the last thing I had expected. Moreover, I was supposed to keep this a secret from Jack because they didn't want him to be "unnecessarily stressed." Little did they know that we had spent the last several weeks learning how to be candid with one another, and secrets of any kind were now outlawed. I felt as though I had been punched in the solar plexus. The nightmare scenario had returned with a vengeance.

I managed to keep this secret for about twenty-four hours, operating as if disconnected from the earth. Then it all burst out. "The doctor told me not to tell you, but I can't help it. Your tumor has started to grow back, fast, and they are worried. How could I keep that a secret?"

Jack admitted that his first reaction was a feeling of panic, but it only lasted a few seconds. After that, his old pragmatic optimism came to the fore. "I'm not dead yet, or even dying, so maybe we should try another approach."

The Janker Klinik also decided to try a different approach, and the doctors told Jack that he needed to stay in the clinic for a few days while they changed his chemotherapy regimen. No more "Disappearing American" act. The new protocol would begin on Monday. In the meantime, we had made plans for the weekend.

CHAPTER FOURTEEN
Artes for Healing

We had tried to economize during the several weeks of our stay at the Hotel Esplanade by choosing a room without a bath. Since we shared the communal bathroom with only one other guest room, this was hardly a privation. Outside the bathroom there was a simple wooden chest on which people had placed unwanted reading materials. It didn't take Jack long to discover a catalog for a German wholesaler of fine art prints called *Artes*. The catalogue accompanied Jack on many happy trips to the "reading room," and he began to show me pictures of some of the prints that appealed to him, like the brilliant colors of the Japanese artist Ay-O, the "rainbow man," and the fantastic shapes of the Expressionist artist Friedensreich Hundertwasser. We found out that the headquarters of *Artes* was located in Rheda, just an hour's train ride from Bonn.

Jack and I had always shared a love of art and had long since decided that fine art prints, such as etchings, lithographs, and woodblocks, gave the most beauty for the money. Our collection was in its fledgling stage in those days, but growing, since we often gave each other a print for Christmas or birthdays.

Now, having received what amounted to another death sentence—this time by the German doctors—we decided to take a trip to Rheda before the new, intensive dose of chemotherapy. We had no visions of what the future would bring, no feelings of desperation or wanting a last fling. We just wanted to go and look at some beautiful art. So on the weekend before the new regimen was to begin, we hopped on a train to Cologne, then changed to a modest little electric train, disembarking at the kind of German country town that you'd imagine would specialize in cheeses. The baroque Artes building was one of the grandest in town. We were greeted cordially and given a tour of the relatively small exhibit space. Quickly, we settled on two prints that were a good value at the time, and ultimately, would be among the most valuable prints we would ever have. We knew they were a luxury that we probably couldn't afford, but we didn't care.

One of the prints was an op-art abstract by the Hungarian-French artist Victor Vasarely and the other an abstract floral still life by the French artist Claude Gaveau. The Vasarely hung over our living room sofa for years, until we eventually decided to make room for other less known, but equally intriguing works, by donating it to the

Portland Art Museum. The Gaveau continues to hang in my bedroom as a reminder of the day Jack and I took that rickety little train to Rheda and traded all our thoughts of death by cancer for a vibrant world of art. Later, Jack would say repeatedly that he thought beauty was one of the most important ingredients in the healing process.

CHAPTER FIFTEEN
An Introduction to Spiritual Healing

So Jack moved away from the comforts of the Hotel Esplanade and our doting host, Ben, and away from my bed into a narrow bed in the Janker Klinik. This time, they put him in a private room at the end of the hall while they socked him with heavy-duty chemicals. It was one of the few times that he really did feel sick.

Jack's new room in the clinic is indelibly fixed in my memory, not so much because it felt, even smelled, like the reality of cancer, but because of the picture that hung over his bed. It was a reproduction of an old Flemish still life with a bowl of fruit, a wine decanter and glass, and a dead goose whose head, on its long neck, lolled over the side of the table. So much for the Janker Klinik's idea of hospital art!

The chemotherapy seemed at least as powerful as the type he'd had at NIH. Jack's resulting lethargy and gray complexion were vivid reminders that our lighthearted days were over, and once again, we were dealing with the proximity of death.

That Monday when I went up the hill for my German lesson, I broke down and told Udo what was happening. He listened intently, then wrote down two names. The first was a woman who was a Christian Science practitioner, who Udo believed would be able to see us right away. The second name was Frau Anni Ziemer, a renowned spiritual healer, with whom he said it would be difficult to get an appointment, but that he and Anke would see what they could do.

We called the Christian Science healer that night and made an appointment to see her a couple days later. On Wednesday, Jack was well enough to go out, and we took a taxi to the woman's address. Fortunately, she spoke English, asked us several questions, and listened in a dreamy, detached sort of way. When it was time to go, she led us to the door with such a slow and controlled manner that I remember having the impression that she was blind, although we never found out if that was the case. We left feeling disappointed, although we hadn't really known what to expect.

At my German lesson the next day, Udo seemed distracted. A man whom I had not seen before was in the apartment, and he and Udo were having a heated conversation. When I told Udo that the Christian Science healer had not been particularly helpful, he seemed annoyed or at least preoccupied, and I felt as though

I was becoming a burden. It was as if he had enough troubles of his own, and here came this distraught American woman begging for help. I could hardly concentrate on German grammar in my desolation. I felt as though the world had abandoned me.

Before I left, Udo said that I should write a letter to Frau Anni Ziemer, and then he would try to follow up. I telephoned him that evening, and he helped me draft the letter, which I sent the next day. Udo then contacted Frau Anni and told her it was an emergency and that we were preparing to leave Germany shortly. Thankfully, she agreed to see us.

Frau Anni lived in Bad Godesberg, the large suburb of Bonn that housed most of the government buildings and embassies. Her office, however, consisted of two small rooms in a modest home. We arrived by taxi at 2:00 p.m. and seated ourselves in her small waiting room. A little table held a few magazines in German, and on the wall was a picture of a distinguished looking, white-haired man.

"That can't be Frau Anni, is it?" Jack asked. I shushed him, but giggled. We were both nervous and wondering what we had gotten ourselves into now.

"No, the caption reads Harry Edwards."

"Who on earth is he?"

Later, we found out that Harry Edwards was an English spiritual healer, one of the great healers of the modern age, and Frau Anni's teacher.

The door to the inner room opened, and we met an elderly, round-faced woman with a halo of white hair. She apologized for her lack of English, but was able to communicate with us in simple sentences, thanks to her studies in England many years ago with the master, Harry Edwards. Frau Anni introduced us to her assistant, who did not speak because his larynx had been removed in a cancer operation. He smiled warmly and shook our hands, and I noticed that he made no effort to hide the open stoma in his neck.

Frau Anni motioned Jack to a chair in the middle of the small room. "I welcome you. You have told us about your situation in your letter. Do you have chemotherapy?"

"Yes."

"Do you have radiation?"

"Yes."

"Oh, that is too bad," Frau Anni said. "The body is difficult to recover from radiation. The damage is permanent."

"The treatment is now finished," Jack replied.

"Well, we see what we can do. Is it permitted to touch you?"

"Of course."

Frau Anni and her assistant then put their hands gently on Jack's body, concentrating on his torso, upper arms, and head. At times she spoke softly in German, not so much to her assistant, but more like prayer. Sometimes, their eyes would be open, looking at Jack, at other times, closed.

The whole scene was so peaceful, so serene, I felt as if benign spirits inhabited the room, all of them telling us that somehow, everything would be all right. After about ten minutes, Frau Anni said the session was over, but that they would continue to send absent healing to Jack every day around noon. At the corresponding time, Jack should sit in meditation wherever he was, and open himself to their healing.

We thanked her, and when I offered, somewhat embarrassed, to pay them, she refused graciously.

"But how do you live, then?" I asked, because it was clear that healing was what they did all day.

"There are people who support us. Don't worry."

We left in a kind of daze, both of us deeply touched by the kindness of this woman and by the almost mysterious power of her presence. Even though she looked quite ordinary, like anyone's grandmother, it was clear she possessed some kind of special energy.

When we got back to the hotel, we sat for a while at a little table in the corner of our room. At one point, I reached over Jack's head to open the casement window. In the process, my hand passed through something in the air that startled me. I could feel something strange, diaphanous, like an energy field, although I had never known what an energy field was or felt like. But there it was, going straight up from the top of his head. As I passed my hand through it, I could feel its edge on either side, and as I raised my hand, I could feel how this energy extended some three feet above his head. I couldn't see it at all, but I could definitely feel it.

I screamed.

"What the hell!" Jack responded.

So I told him, and we both stared at each other in wonder and awe.

CHAPTER SIXTEEN
Live Cell Therapy

Jack's treatment at the Janker Klinik was over. The doctors made it clear there was nothing more they could do at this time, and we should all just hope that the final onslaught of chemotherapy would help. However, it was also clear they didn't expect a cure. Dr. Scheef met with us for an exit interview and gave Jack a starting megadose of vitamin A, which he was to take for several weeks after we returned to Washington, D.C. under the supervision of Dr. Schildwaechter. Each daily dose was nearly one million units. Feeling ambivalent about the effectiveness of that last round of chemotherapy, we were glad they were giving him *something* to continue with after the conventional treatment was stopped. Little did we know about the consequences of too much of a good thing.

Before we left, we had one last dinner with Anke and Udo at our favorite Italian restaurant. That is when we learned about the amazing history and activities of Frau

Anni Ziemer. Germany, like many other countries, has been much more open to alternative healing than the U.S. Sometimes, German patients would ask for a spiritual healer to be present in the operating room during surgery. When the German doctors needed help, it was not unusual for them to call on spiritual healers. In fact, Frau Anni spent a good deal of time traveling around Germany as an invited lecturer in medical schools. As president of the German Association for Spiritual Healing, she was indeed the grande dame of that community. We understood more than ever how fortunate we were to have gotten an appointment with her. When I told Anke and Udo about my experience with the column of energy above Jack's head, they were not at all surprised.

It was nearly the middle of October when we said farewell to Anke and Udo, to Ben and Jana, the Hotel Esplanade, the Janker Klinik, and the city of Bonn, which had become a second home to us for four months. I wondered if we would ever see them again, and, if so, whether it would be both of us, or just one.

From Bonn, we were scheduled to go to Hannover for a treatment Dr. Schildwaechter had arranged. We had a ton of luggage with us this time because of the items we had collected over the months. Since the exchange rate had been nearly three marks to the dollar, we had engaged in a lot of guilt-free shopping. Because some of the clothes we bought were so well made and classically styled, I still wear them nearly thirty years later. Thankfully, Ben drove us to the station. Somehow, we managed to change trains in Cologne and arrived in Hannover late in the afternoon.

Hannover was quite a bit larger than Bonn, and right away I missed the relaxed atmosphere of Bonn. Hannover was more in the style of north German business and industry, and it lacked the Rhine town, historic and romantic ambience. Because Hannover was an important road junction and rail terminus, most of the city center had been badly bombed during World War II. But the results of the rebuilding were not as friendly and graceful as they were in Bonn. We set about exploring the several pedestrian ways, made attractive with trees and greenery in planters, but homesickness clouded my perceptions. I wanted either to be back in Bonn or to be home. New places had lost their appeal.

Dr. Schildwaechter had set us up with an appointment at the Paracelsus Clinic for what he called "live cell therapy" to be administered by clinic medical staff in his absence. This treatment developed by Professor Paul Niehans in the 1930s, had been known as rejuvenation therapy. Famous actors and statesmen had gone to Switzerland and later, to Germany for it. These had included such notables as Winston Churchill, Pope Pius XII, and Gloria Swanson. The treatment involved taking live cells from the fetus of a healthy strain of mountain sheep, and injecting them into human patients. People with liver disease received mainly liver cells, those with heart disease received heart cells, and so forth, depending upon one's weakness or malady. The treatment had only recently been applied to cancer patients, and in that sense, Jack was a guinea pig. We knew nothing about live cell treatment, and we didn't have time before leaving to research the scientific justification, of which there was little, which we discovered later. We decided to trust Dr. Schildwaechter's recommendation that this therapy would be effective, or at least, not harmful.

The day before the cell therapy treatment, we had to have blood tests. I say "we" because Dr. Schildwaechter thought it would be a good idea for me to have a variation of the treatment myself. For years, I had had difficulty tolerating exercise, not during the vigorous walking, hiking, or swimming I liked to do, but afterward when I would feel very tired or even ill for days. So, we both went to a small clinic not far from our hotel to have our blood drawn. Jack's blood was fairly easy to draw, but my veins were thin and uncooperative, and the technician was so exasperated that I felt like a terrible patient. After the first technician dealt with me and both arms felt like pin cushions, another technician finally drew the blood from my hands. Again, I was homesick for our gentle treatment in Bonn.

We stayed in the large, modern Hotel am Stadtpark, and the medical staff came to our room to administer the injections. At the time, it didn't occur to us that a hotel was a strange type of "clinic." The medical staff gave Jack several large syringes of a gray viscous fluid, and I was given one. Jack's dose was so strong that his usually resilient body reacted, and he had to bolt for the bathroom, weak and trembling.

"Go in with him," the doctor ordered, so I complied and held on to him while he had copious diarrhea.

"There goes the romance," was Jack's only comment.

The doctors had told us that we were to rest in our room for two days and not to get out of bed for anything except to go to the bathroom and to answer the door when room service delivered our meals. Fortunately, we had stocked up with videos (in English, for the benefit of the international clientele), and we sat through two viewings of Tootsie, which we had already seen. It was just as funny the third time as it was the first.

At the end of the second day, we were bored and restless, so we slipped out and walked to a nearby restaurant we had noticed the day before the treatment. It was called the Budweiserhaus, a name Jack said originated in Germany not St. Louis, and had the best meal of our entire German experience. We feasted on paté, venison with boysenberry relish, glazed carrots, scalloped potatoes, wine, chocolate cake, and coffee, with no adverse consequences. We knew that if we could handle that meal, we were both in pretty good shape.

The next day at breakfast, we spied Dr. Schildwaechter in the dining room.

"What's he doing here?" I whispered to Jack. "He told us that he wasn't able to come."

Dr. Schildwaechter came over to our table and greeted us cordially, telling us that he had come to Hannover for some kind of meeting. We were surprised that he had not been there for the administration of the treatment. This was the first of several instances where the accountability of the mysterious Dr. Schildwaechter came into question.

In retrospect, I question whether there actually *was* a Paracelsus Clinic in Hannover. We never received any official prescriptions or receipts, only flyers consisting of rudimentary information on cheap colored paper labeled Continental Health Clinics, Ltd. Dr. Schildwaechter had given us these homemade flyers, along with a statement of his $4,250 fee—quite a sum at that time. There was, and still is, a Paracelsus Clinic in Switzerland, but Germany banned the administration of live cell therapy in 1997 because of its potentially dangerous side effects. The Swiss clinics, however, are still in business.

Live-cell therapy such as the type we experienced should not be confused with contemporary stem cell therapy derived from human tissue. Instead, the injection of live cells from animal fetuses has been condemned by much of the Western medical establishment, including the American Cancer Society, because of the absence of scientific evidence of its success, and because of its serious risks, including severe allergic reactions and even death. Whether we would have risked it knowing this information is an open question. I certainly would not have chosen it for myself, but Jack, with his dire prognosis, was open to most anything.

The next day we traveled, once again, on the smooth and punctual German trains headed for Brussels, Oostende, Dover, London, and, finally, via British Air back to Washington D.C. At last, we were home with our friends and family, and our beloved Max who had nearly died of a broken heart until Lou, our saintly house-and-dog-sitter, had decided to take Max to work with him every day. A mountain of unpaid bills and junk mail greeted us, as did Barbara our intrepid therapist. A rigorous and imaginative healing program awaited us—more than I could ever have anticipated.

CHAPTER SEVENTEEN
Into the Fire

Barbara made room for us in her schedule right away, and we started our weekly couples' therapy. Before each session, she would see us each individually, and it was gratifying for me to have someone focus on *my* troubles and *my* feelings. It had seemed to me that everybody always focused on Jack and was indifferent to my needs. Sometimes, I felt invisible. Barbara helped me to be more outspoken about my own feelings, a lesson I believed to be difficult. In time, I learned to speak up fairly well, at least with her. Once during a couple's session, I complained that nobody was listening to me, only to Jack, and she replied, "On the contrary, I believe I spend more time responding to you than to him."

Actually, she was quite right. I felt needy and I was letting her know. However, it was a bit more difficult asking for help from my family and friends.

In these sessions, Barbara led us through the prickly maze of fears, resentments, and disappointments that had characterized our relationship. But by the end of every session, she always guided us to the unshakable foundation of love that lay beneath it all. Sometimes, the process would take as long as two hours, and, as often as not there would be a restless client waiting in her living room.

I think Barbara considered us an emergency even though she didn't refer to us that way. More than once she squeezed us into her busy schedule and even saw us on the spur of the moment. When she decided that a particular activity would be good for us, she let us know in no uncertain terms. Behind her soft drawl, "I think it would be a good idea if y'all did_____," was an aspect of steel. If she suggested it, we were to do it. In most instances, we complied without hesitation. She knew, as we did, that there was no time to waste.

Despite the gloomy prognosis, when we left Germany Jack continued to feel and look well, and he went back to work part-time. He was not in any pain or even discomfort, and he seemed to have plenty of energy for whatever Barbara recommended, as well as his own activities. He was especially eager for those healing activities that felt good to him, like massage and the acupressure I supplied.

On Barbara's recommendation, we took meditation lessons from her boyfriend, Ed. Actually, we both had begun to meditate in Germany, but more instruction in meditation certainly didn't hurt. In fact, we had read about the possibility of contacting one's spirit guide during meditation. One day while Jack was meditating in Germany, he felt as though he met his spirit guide, the improbable image of a man in a gray business suit named Ken. I never did hear what Ken was guiding Jack to do, or for that matter, anything more about him. Later, it was a source of amusement for both of us, this image that was so different from Jack's.

Ed gave each of us a mantra, and we both found value in our own personal versions of meditation, which Jack and I continued for years. Our meditations were reinforced and expanded through workshops with Jim Green, a retired sociologist and U.S. Agency for International Development official turned spiritual counselor and meditation teacher, whose practices I still use on a daily basis. Often, these periods of quiet contemplation would turn into to-do lists or "monkey mind" chatter, but we would stay at it for at least 30 minutes, and usually feel refreshed afterward. Sometimes, Jack would go to sleep. Barbara told us not to judge our meditations, but just to stay committed to the process.

Barbara also recommended that we join her therapy group for couples that met every other week. In addition, Jack joined another of Barbara's groups for singles, which he found valuable. So, he was having some kind of therapy nearly every day. The couples group, which we endured for several months, was not the high point of our therapeutic experience, and we agreed that Barbara's talents were better displayed in our private sessions as individuals and as a couple. It seemed that our

group was a haven for passive-aggressive men who elic-
ited rage, not only from their wives, but from all the rest of
us. At least I felt free to display my unhappiness with the
process to the group, which felt like a new level of candor.

In other respects, however, Barbara's recommendations were invaluable. One of the most daunting,
but certainly memorable, was fire walking. Barbara
thought it would be a good idea for Jack to engage
in an activity that would bring home the body-mind
connection, something during which he could experience firsthand the power of his mind. She also thought
it would be a good idea for me to share the experience—
literally—not just as a bystander.

I had heard of people walking on hot coals, and I
had always thought of it in the same category as sword
swallowing and levitating, and even more reckless and
bizarre than jumping out of airplanes. It had never
occurred to me to try any of it. But if Barbara recommended fire walking (ordered was more like it), we complied. So, we went to a large house in Potomac, an upscale
suburb of D.C. Our group included several people whom
we didn't know, some of whom were other clients of
Barbara's. Jack had told the children about this, and to
my surprise, our son, Robert, wanted to come along. I
wasn't sure if he intended to actually do the fire walk or
just wanted to watch. I don't imagine he was sure either.

By the time we arrived, it was already dark, but I
could see the bonfire burning in the backyard. For at

least two hours we sat in the living room, listening to a lecture and meditating. The lecturer was a gentle Buddhist who talked in an almost hypnotic way about the power of intention, how fire can burn when we resist it or when it touches us accidentally, but not when we confront it willingly. In retrospect, I'm reminded of the Cathar martyrs in southern France, who, when finally captured by the pope's crusaders and condemned to burn at the stake, walked into the fire singing. It's not as if they weren't incinerated, but they gave themselves willingly and fearlessly.

When our leader decided that we had prepared sufficiently and the coals were at the right stage (glowing but not in flames), he took us into the backyard and we removed our shoes. Then we circled the fire several times and spoke to it with statements like:

"Fire, you are my friend."

"I am strong. I am ready for this encounter."

"Hot coals, I am not afraid of you."

The plan was to walk across a bed of hot coals about three feet long. Our leader went first, relaxed, stepping easily along the glowing path. Then Barbara crossed, swinging her arms and dancing, turning around at one point, then turning back. After a while, Jack crossed, not exactly gracefully, but confident and unhurried. Then Robert stepped forward and, arms held high, his long bleached-blonde curls flowing, strode across the coals. Later, he strode across again! I was awed.

When it was my turn, I was anything but fearless. I was terrified, but determined—not only to face the coals but also not to be the family coward. I would say that I walked the coals to support Jack, but I think the stronger motivation was pride. At any rate, I hustled through those three feet of hot coals, and they felt hot indeed. Afterward, when I examined my feet, there were some small red marks, certainly not blisters, and not even burns, but evidence of the encounter. The feet of both Jack and Robert were lily white.

CHAPTER EIGHTEEN
Less Conventional All the Time

In addition to the therapy with Barbara, Jack began to see another therapist named Caroline Sperling. Our pharmacist recommended Caroline as a former cancer patient herself, and Jack just thought that more and deeper would be even better, which turned out to be true. Caroline specialized in cancer counseling and used a method called New Identity Process Therapy. The idea behind this therapeutic approach was to bring out painful repressed emotions and release them physically in the presence of a caring therapist. This process would then make room for positive emotions and beliefs.

Members of Caroline's therapy group would talk for a while in the group and then go downstairs to her rec room, which was equipped with yoga mats and tennis rackets. The participants would beat on the mats with the tennis rackets, yelling and screaming whatever they felt like. Afterward, they would pair up, lay down on the mats, and hug each other, taking turns yelling or sobbing, or just talking. There was nothing sexual about it. People paired up with same-sex partners or opposite-sex partners—it didn't matter. Jack always came home after those sessions feeling relaxed and relieved.

Therapy sessions with Barbara and Caroline were not the only healing activities Jack engaged in. I still gave him acupressure every day, which was always calming for me as well as for him, especially after a day of worry about work, money, or our relationship. We had ordered some tapes by the author and motivational speaker Louise Hay speaking about the powers of the body and mind to heal, and we often played them during the acupressure sessions. Author of the *New York Times* bestseller, *You Can Heal Your Life,* Louise Hay was one of the early popular proponents of the body-mind connection. Having been diagnosed with "incurable" cervical cancer in the 1970s, she refused conventional treatment in favor of a regimen based on for-giveness, psychotherapy, nutrition, and other unconven-tional healing methods. She is especially well known for advocating healing affirmations to be repeated over and over throughout the day. When we listened to her tapes, Jack and I were always comforted by her mellifluous voice making statements like: "Be kind to yourself. Love and approve of yourself." I particularly liked: "Would you rather be happy and well, or would you rather be right?"

Jack also started having Reiki sessions, a hands-on healing technique developed by a Japanese monk in the 1920s in which the healer places his or her palms on specific spots on the patient's body, transferring qi (energy) from healer to patient. By the 1980s, Reiki had become a popular alternative or supplemental healing practice, sometimes used by nurses as well as by interested lay healers.

In addition, Barbara told us about a kind of healing called *Johrei,* another meditative type of healing based on the principle of energy exchange similar to Reiki and acupressure. The person giving Johrei would hold her hand close to the recipient, not touching him, and focus her mind to visualize energy entering her own head flowing through her body, down her arm, out her upraised hand, and into the body of the recipient. We went twice monthly to Johrei meetings at a house in nearby Wheaton, Maryland.

Like Reiki, Johrei was also developed in Japan. Its founder, Mokichi Okada, was very much in tune with the beauty of nature and, in addition to his system of spiritual healing, developed principles of organic farming. Many of the Johrei practitioners also emigrated from Japan to Brazil in the 1950s and 1960s at the invitation of the Brazilian government because Brazil had a shortage of doctors. The flexible Brazilians were always ready to embrace a variety of spiritual paths. It turned out that most of the people at our Johrei meetings in Wheaton were Brazilians employed by the embassy in Washington.

For many years, Jack felt as though he had some kind of karmic connection with Japan. Throughout our life together he bought several Japanese prints, took Ikebana lessons, and had a large collection of Japanese tea bowls. Unfortunately, we never did visit Japan together, although we always talked about the possibility. Jack was an ideal recipient of all kinds of massage and bodywork, especially of the Japanese variety, and positively soaked up the energy from all these activities. He actually became a practitioner of Johrei, and people whom he worked on would often comment to me that they felt powerful energy coming from him.

Even though we were both working, we managed to find time for our therapy sessions and all our various healing activities: acupressure, reflexology, Reiki, and Johrei. Jack was also getting regular massages. He engaged in even more of these activities than I did, and his schedule read like a debutante's dance card. We had left Germany with an ominous prognosis and that fact lingered in our minds, but we were too busy to let it take us down. Jack was still feeling strong, in reasonably good spirits, and the psychotherapy kept us both focused on the task at hand. He was determined to meet this challenge head-on and do everything he could to beat it, especially if those activities felt good. He used to say that he was just a sponge for bodywork, but we were well aware that conventional medicine was no longer part of Jack's protocol. We felt that both the Janker Klinik and the NIH had exhausted their options.

One day about three months after our return from Germany, I got a breathless phone call from my friend Donna, the woman who had taught me foot reflexology. She was also the one who had loaned me the depressing textbook that said esophageal cancer is fatal in virtually every case. Donna had just received a routine visit from her friend Christine, who had given her a psychic reading. At the end of their session, Christine remarked, almost as an afterthought as she was going out the door, "You have a friend with cancer. Tell him his cancer is gone, but he must continue his meditation and visualization for the rest of his life!"

"Donna," I said, "what had you told her about Jack?"

"Nothing! I told her nothing."

"But Donna, how did she know you had a friend with...."

"Nothing! I told her nothing. She's psychic, remember?"

I was astonished. Jack wasn't home, so I called my friend Anne, always a sensible, sometimes even literal, personality. She listened, then responded, "Congratulations!"

When I told Jack, he looked at me intently, then just smiled. "I thought so."

CHAPTER NINETEEN
Alcohol

You would think that the good news from Donna's psychic friend Christine would have had a major impact on our lives. It was heartening for a while, but that sense of well-being didn't last very long. It's true we were uninterested in any more conventional medicine—no more CT scans, x-rays, or even blood tests. By this time, Jack was seeing Dr. Schildwaechter regularly, taking all kinds of expensive enzymes and vitamins, and continuing with his megadoses of vitamin A. Our lives were so focused on psychotherapy and various personal growth and healing activities that we didn't have the time or energy to consider whether or not Christine was correct. Nor did we worry about whether the other healing activities were working, or if we should change our diet or do something else. We continued all the healing activities, but the main focus was psychotherapy and our relationship, in addition to the practical aspects of our lives, such as work, finances, and children.

Jack was feeling well enough to work as a cabinetmaker's assistant with two carpenters to whom he became devoted: Charlie, mature and wise, (whose friendship lasted for many years), and John, a lovable gap-toothed hell-raiser who seemed to spend a lot of time taking driver's ed because he was repeatedly convicted of a DUI and he never seemed to have a valid driver's license when pulled over.

Jack spent his off-hours making furniture and decorative items in his woodworking shop in the basement. He created many fine pieces, including Japanese tansu chests complete with authentic hardware, folding library ladders styled after a design by Thomas Jefferson, and beautiful music stands. He sold a few of them, but most he kept or just gave away. Many of these pieces I still cherish today.

One day, I discovered an open, half-gallon bottle of wine in the basement. In fact, it had seemed as if Jack's breath smelled like wine a good deal of the time, and now that he wasn't smoking cigars anymore, it was unmistakable. At every meal he would have several glasses of wine, and I finally realized he had been in a mild state of inebriation much of the past several years. At the very least, he was under the influence.

He'd given up the strong stuff—martinis and scotch— years ago. Now, it was just wine, but alcohol nevertheless, and enough to take the edge off life's rough places. If a therapy session had been tough and he had to deal with my anger along with his guilt and resentment, a few glasses of wine would soften it. If the kids were acting out, wine would make it tolerable. He was never abusive or even argumentative. Jack's love for me and for the kids was never in question, although they were nervous with his driving. But alcohol also made him remote and unresponsive. I used to accuse him of being Alfred E. Neuman of *Mad* magazine. What? Me worry? Nothing seemed to bother Jack when he would be in that place.

Thinking about this many years later, it amazes me that his drinking never came out in our therapy sessions. I would be infuriated by his passivity, but the role of alcohol never came up. Now, I wonder how I could ever have been so naïve. I also wonder how Barbara couldn't have suspected it, because if she had, she surely would have brought it up.

A friend had given me a book called *Passive Men, Wild Women* by the psychiatrist Pierre Mornell that described so well the condition in which passive-aggressive men invoke the screaming banshee in otherwise reasonable women. That's what I thought it was, passive aggression. But when the truth of his alcoholism flew straight into my face, I realized Frank Schaefer had been right and I had been in denial all those years. It wasn't so much passive aggressive behavior as it was alcoholic zoning out. It was one of the most common and universal ways of dealing with pain. Jack was not cutting back on his drinking as he had promised, but instead had taken it underground. Not only did I realize the deadening effect on our relationship, but I feared the alcohol would weaken his immune system and lead to a recurrence of the cancer. I knew I had to do something drastic, no matter how scary or painful, and I was beginning to feel desperate.

So one night after we had finished dinner, I confronted him with the bottle in the basement, along with my frustration, worry, and desolation. I told him he either had to quit drinking entirely or I would leave him. He never hesitated. He poured out the remainder of any open bottle and went to Alcoholics Anonymous a couple of days later. That day in January was the last taste of alcohol he had for several years.

Later, when Jack began to drink a little wine again, he drank only when socializing. If we were out to dinner with friends, he'd only have two or three glasses of wine, but it was no longer a problem for him to control. Jack concluded that although he had been psychologically dependent upon alcohol, he was not chemically addicted, which made it much less painful to give up. After two AA meetings, he decided the program wasn't for him and that he could just quit cold turkey. He did, however, refer to himself as an alcoholic in true AA fashion.

For the first few weeks after Jack stopped drinking, it was a bit unsettling. For a while, I kept on having a glass or two of wine with dinner, and he didn't seem to mind. But it was different having somebody who used to be relatively remote, now be more present with me and with everyone. Occasionally, it almost felt like he was in my face, which was disconcerting.

Barbara told me that sometimes when a partner stops drinking, the change can be so abrupt that the spouse almost wishes they would go back to drinking again. Gradually, Jack and I became closer and more authentic with each other. He was more willing to stand up to me, to be a fully participating partner, and to deal with life's daily problems. In turn, I was grateful for what he had been willing to do and how it had begun to transform our relationship.

CHAPTER TWENTY
Vitamin A:
Too Much of a Good Thing

By February 1986, four months after we had returned from Germany, things were looking up. Although we still didn't know the status of the tumor—if any tumor still existed, we just kept on with what we were doing. We continued with intensive psychotherapy, personal growth seminars, Reiki, Johrei, acupressure, reflexology, and treatments with Dr. Schildwaechter. These treatments included several kinds of enzymes with names like Cytozyme, Rentenzyme, Fe-zyme, Intenzyme, Lysozyme, and Placenta, in addition to multi-vitamins and various other supplements such as magnesium, selenium, and Coenzyme Q10. There was also something called Resistocell that Dr. Schildwaechter periodically injected in Jack. He took all of this daily, in addition to the megadose of vitamin A—nearly one million units per day.

As the months passed and there was no overt sign of cancer, we began to think that it was *really* gone. However, there was one unsettling sign: Jack was slowly losing weight. Along with that came a slightly sallow complexion, and after a while, weakness in his arms and legs. His everyday chores became difficult. After several months, Jack was just dragging himself around and had become alarmingly thin. When he would ask Dr. Schildwaechter what was wrong, his questions were evaded.

One of the things I had learned over several months was to do "muscle testing," also known as applied kinesiology. Jack would hold his right arm straight out, and I would press on it, trying to push it down as he resisted my pressure. Then I would have him make a test statement like "I should change jobs." If his arm stayed strong, the answer was yes; if it was pushed down easily, the answer would be no. It was the body's way (or that of the subconscious) to provide information. This is how Jack and I tried to figure out what was wrong.

Admittedly, it was more than a little unorthodox, but we were completely disenchanted with mainstream medicine, and Dr. Schildwaechter wasn't providing answers. So, Jack would stand with his arm outstretched and say, "I am free of cancer," and his arm would remain rigid. Then, because I had long been concerned about the amount of vitamin A he was taking, I asked him to say, "I need vitamin A." With that, his arm flopped down.

That afternoon at our session with Barbara, I told her the results of our muscle testing and expressed frustration over how Dr. Schildwaechter equivocated. In true Barbara style, she looked up his phone number and handed me the phone. I was the one who expressed the worry, so I got the phone. At that point, Jack was too weak to engage in what he knew would be a fight, so he relied more than ever on my leadership. I dialed Dr. Schildwaechter on the spot. His assistant answered the phone, and I told her that I had a very important question for the doctor. When Dr. Schildwaechter came to the phone, I told him that I was terribly concerned about Jack's symptoms, about the huge quantities of vitamin A he had been taking, and that I suspected a connection. Furthermore, muscle testing showed Jack's body didn't need it. I knew that Dr. Schildwaechter accepted muscle testing as a useful diagnostic tool.

He replied, "Well, one part of his body may not need it, but another part definitely does. He should keep on taking it."

I was exasperated, and Jack was also upset, but we felt like we had burned all other bridges and Dr. Schildwaechter's treatment was the only alternative. Although we didn't discuss it, there was the alternative of stopping all treatment and letting his body heal itself. But we were both afraid to trust our own instincts, even though we were rapidly losing faith in Dr. Schildwaechter.

Jack continued to take nearly a million units of vitamin A every day. By now it had been almost a year since Jack had left the Janker Klinik and began taking this megadose. As summer wore into fall, Jack grew progressively weaker and developed a host of alarming symptoms. He started to have pains in his shoulders and cramps in his legs and hands, his skin became itchy and chapped, and he lost facial and body hair. Not being familiar with the symptoms of Vitamin A intoxication, we began to think the cancer had returned.

Since we had no conventional doctor and no longer trusted Dr. Schildwaechter, we didn't know what to do. Finally, we felt that the only option that made any sense was to return to the Janker Klinik. So, once again we prepared for the trip to Bonn. This time, instead of taking the usual route with so many changes, we decided to fly Icelandic Air directly from Washington D.C. to Luxembourg, where we would take the bus to Cologne, then the train to Bonn. Before we left, Barbara contacted her friend, the healer George Chapman in Wales, who agreed to see us on our way back.

The flight was uneventful, and it was good not to have to do the London–Dover–Oostende–Cologne–Bonn trek when Jack was so weak. Jack had taken off his shoes on the plane and found to his dismay that his feet had swelled so much during the journey that he couldn't get his shoes back on. So he wore his slipper-socks all the way from Luxembourg City to Bonn. It must have been a strange sight to see this tall, gaunt man shuffling down the street in bedroom slippers carrying luggage.

Once we reached Bonn, we sank into the comfort of the Esplanade where Ben and Jana greeted us warmly. It was almost like being home again, and reassuring to be close to a medical establishment with doctors we trusted.

The next day we met with Dr. Scheef, the clinic director. After examining Jack, we thought he said, "It *must* not be cancer." We were startled. Then it became clear that in the translation from German to English, the word "muss" also meant "need." So, he was saying, "It *need* not be cancer." Even then, the news was heartening.

Unlike the slow turn around time on test results at American medical establishments, including the great NIH, the CT scan results at the Janker Klinik came back quickly. There was no sign of cancer. But Dr. Scheef had already made his diagnosis, which he was now free to share with us: vitamin A poisoning.

In fact, Dr. Scheef told us that he had tried some of his own protocols on himself, and when he was considering the administration of megadoses of vitamin A after treatment with chemotherapy, he had concluded that a couple of months should be the *maximum*. After two months at this dose, Dr. Scheef had grown so weak he was hardly able to lift himself out of his car—a racy little Porsche as it turned out. By now, Jack had survived a whole year of this brutal treatment, and his liver had been badly damaged. Afterward, Jack was fond of saying that he had probably ingested more vitamin A than any human being who lived to tell.

Dr. Scheef immediately took him off vitamin A and started him on the diuretic Aldactone. Jack responded well, gaining strength within just a few days. We were overjoyed.

CHAPTER TWENTY-ONE
The English Psychic

Once we had the good news from the Janker Klinik, we knew we could go home with light hearts. Before we left, we had dinner with Anke and Udo in our favorite Italian restaurant, and they offered to take us to a presentation by an English psychic named Gaye Muir. They also were interested in matters of the spirit and the body-mind-spirit connection, and were knowledgeable about the spiritual healing community in Europe. The previous year, they had referred us to the awe inspiring Frau Anni Ziemer. Anke and Udo had taken Anke's great aunt, who was suffering from arthritis, to see Mrs. Muir. During the session, Mrs. Muir had put the woman in contact with her late husband and a childhood playmate. The aunt's arthritis seemed to be better after the encounter.

The event with Gaye Muir took place in a high school auditorium in Sieburg, a suburb of Bonn. It was a big gathering, probably more than 300 people. We sat close to the front on the left side, and I was immediately disconcerted by an unpleasant crackling of the amplification system accompanied by the occasional blinking of some of the house lights. After a while, a matronly middle-aged woman came out and addressed us in English.

"Don't be surprised by all the static," she said. "It's only energy."

"What on earth?" I whispered to Jack, already skeptical with the whole scene.

Then Mrs. Muir asked for an interpreter. There was muttering in the audience as if people were wondering why she hadn't thought of this before. Finally, a young woman stepped up to the microphone and agreed to translate into German.

Mrs. Muir explained that she was able to see spirits hovering around members of the audience, and the energy and excitement were generated by their eagerness to communicate with us. She told us that she would identify a spirit and relay its communication to the selected member of the audience. This person was to nod yes if the communication was appropriate, or shake their head for no if it didn't make sense. Initially, some of the communications seemed relatively generic, like a grandmother conveying support to a young woman, or an uncle giving advice to his nephew. Often, the descriptions of these sprits were fairly detailed, such as a woman wearing her hair in a bun or a man with a black mustache. At one point, Mrs.

Muir said to a woman who was sitting near us, "I see a black and white cat."

The woman shook her head to indicate no.

"It's a black and white cat who passed over recently and wants you to know that it's all right."

Again, the woman shook her head for no.

But the woman next to her spoke, *"Das ist mein Katz,"* and began to cry.

Then, to my amazement, Mrs. Muir spoke directly to Jack. "You are here because of your health. You have come a long way to resolve a conflict."

Jack nodded affirmatively.

Mrs. Muir continued, "I see a woman with a very thin upper lip, perhaps an aunt, who loved you like a mother."

My attention was riveted on Jack, whose mouth turned down slightly at the corners, a gesture that was sometimes accompanied by eyes welling up. He said softly, "Aunt Izzy."

It made sense. Jack's mother had died when he was only seven, and Aunt Izzy had stepped into the breach. She and her husband had folded little Jackie and Bobby into their family and gave them the affection and freedom they had failed to receive from their father and stepmother.

Still focused on Jack, Mrs. Muir continued. "I see a young man, a flyer who was killed in the war. He is telling you to be strong."

Jack said quietly, "Joe Glenn." Jack had been close friends with Joe's younger brother. Evidently, Joe had flown out into the Pacific on a mission and, like Amelia Earhart, had lost communication and never returned.

Again, Mrs. Muir referred to a spirit hovering around Jack. "Someone fat and balding says you owe him $5." As this was translated, everyone laughed.

Jack nodded again, and explained to me, "That's Meyer, the guy who ran the Sideline." The Sideline was Jack's favorite pub in St. Louis during his college days. "That's just the kind of crack Meyer would make."

After that, Mrs. Muir moved on to other people, but we sat there stunned, grateful that she had selected Jack out of that big crowd of people. We were blown away by the accuracy and relevance of it all. It was also a dramatic testament that, at least when we are in trouble, we are surrounded by forces of love and support, spirits whom we may be completely unaware of in our day-to-day existence.

During the intermission, a woman came up to me and said, "Do you believe in this?"

"Of course." What else could I say with such powerful evidence?

It was October 31, 1986, the eve of All Saints Day.

Once in a while I think back on this event and wonder, *Who is hovering over my shoulder now? Who is trying to tell me that everything will be all right? What voices should I be listening to?*

CHAPTER TWENTY-TWO
Doctor in a Borrowed Body

The next day would be our last in Bonn for nearly fifteen years. Ben, our faithful innkeeper and friend, drove us to Luxembourg City so we could fly back on Icelandic Air. This time, however, we had a long stopover in England because Barbara had arranged an appointment for us with George Chapman and Dr. Lang in Wales.

It was our understanding that the fact Dr. Lang had died in 1935 was really unimportant. Many believed that he continued his work by channeling through a former firefighter named George Chapman. When I first learned about this doctor in spirit, I couldn't help but think, *Who, but Barbara, would have known about this connection?*

Evidently, George Chapman was one of several insufficiently occupied firefighters who used to sit in a circle and dabble in psychic phenomena during the long hours of waiting for emergencies. George had started communicating with people's spirit guides when, one day, he began to speak in a very genteel but authoritative voice. The voice identified itself as William Lang, former president of the British Ophthalmological Society. When other members of the circle were skeptical, Dr. Lang commanded them to do some research to verify his identity. They went to the local library and found nothing about a Dr. Lang. But in the next session, the voice told them to go to the Ophthalmological Society's headquarters in London, which they did, and they discovered that everything the spirit told them was true.

Eventually, George Chapman gave up firefighting and devoted all of his time to Dr. Lang and his patients. Word of his healing abilities spread, and some doctors in London decided to check him out. They found Dr. Lang's living daughter, who attended a séance with George Chapman channeling Dr. Lang. She confirmed her father's identity. After this, word about the healing powers of Chapman/ Lang spread, and people came from afar to see him. British medical doctors even set up a practice for the Chapman/ Lang duo, and referred patients.

Barbara found out about Dr. Lang when she started to have serious problems with her eyes. Physicians at Johns Hopkins Hospital in Baltimore told her at that time that the condition was serious, but they were unable to help her. Being well connected to the alternative network, Barbara had found out about George Chapman/Dr. Lang, and flew over for treatment. Whatever he did, she recovered completely, and while she was in Wales, even went dancing with George Chapman.

None of this was surprising to us. Knowing Barbara, and having had our eyes opened to all kinds of unconventional healing, we were ready to try anything. So, before we had left Washington this time, and not knowing whether or not Jack's cancer had returned, Barbara called George Chapman to set up an appointment.

Our destination was Machynlleth in Wales, a tiny town off the beaten track. We had to take three trains to get there from London. It was late October, and although there was no snow, a winter chill had definitely set in. Our little pension had no heating except a perpetual fire in the parlor where we lingered as long as possible before ascending to our frigid bedroom. Despite the thick stonewalls of the pension, gaping cracks around the windows allowed free passage to the winter air. In our bedroom, the curtains swayed in the breeze. Poor Jack, his blood permanently thinned by chemotherapy and his liver decimated by vitamin A poisoning, was almost cadaverous. At least our innkeeper gave us hot water bottles, which helped for a little while, and I held his shivering body close.

As we huddled around the parlor fire, we perused the hotel's guestbook, and there, big as life, was the name of our friend Frank Schaefer, White Horse Inn, Provincetown, Massachusetts, dated two years earlier. Yet another encounter with the ubiquitous Frank Schaefer during our adventures.

Somehow, we survived the frigid night and set off for George Chapman's house the next morning. The taxi driver had no trouble finding the house as he must have been there hundreds of times before. He let us off in the driveway next to a small building that served as the office, about fifty feet down the hill from a comfortable looking Welsh home. A handsome, middle-aged man came out to welcome us. George Chapman was robust and ruddy cheeked with a slightly graying beard and a firm handshake. He addressed us in a soft northern-English brogue.

"I hope you had a good journey. Please have a seat in the office and Dr. Lang will be out in a little while."

Five people were already seated in the waiting room: an English couple with their young daughter, and two young men from India who, as Jack always liked to say afterward, "looked like they didn't have two rupees to rub together." We were amazed the young men had traveled so far to see Dr. Lang. I wonder if they thought the same about us.

We waited for what seemed like an hour, while the other patients were being attended to. Finally, a young man, who we later learned was George's son, Michael, called us into a heavily curtained, dimly lit, back room. Michael asked me whether I was a friend or the wife. Immediately, we could tell the spirit of Dr. Lang was already there. I was struck by how different his persona was from the George

Chapman we had just met earlier that morning. It was as if George's body had just aged twenty years. He seemed thinner and grayer, and his speech was refined and courtly as he invited us to join him.

Dr. Lang greeted us by shaking Jack's hand and embracing me lightly. "Cheeky, isn't he, asking 'wife or friend'?" he said, referring to Michael. Dr. Lang called Jack by his first name and me by "my dear."

"You have come a long way," we heard once again. After Dr. Lang conversed with Jack for a few minutes, he asked Jack to lie on an examining table and passed his hands over Jack's body. He told us that he was now going to work on Jack's "etheric body," which extended beyond the borders of the physical body we know. While he worked, he talked to someone whom we didn't see and snapped his fingers loudly from time to time.

"There is no cancer," Dr. Lang announced, confirming Dr. Scheef's diagnosis, "but there is a problem with your blood." We had not mentioned the vitamin A poisoning. He continued to pass his hands back and forth over Jack's chest and abdomen and finally told us that Jack would be all right in a while. He then shook Jack's hand and held his cheek briefly to mine, saying that he would check on us in a few days to see how Jack was doing. As we left, I noticed that he squinted in the light of the doorway, almost as if his eyes had been closed.

As with our psychic healer Frau Anni, Dr. Lang/ George Chapman would take no money. Once again, we left feeling that we had been in the presence of a great healer. The fact that Dr. Lang used someone else's body to do his work, that he had actually been physically dead for fifty years, and that he practiced in a little Welsh backwater, detracted not one bit from the power of the experience.

Neither of us had any idea of how this follow-up visit would take place, so we promptly forgot about his promise. Three days later in London, however, Dr. Lang did visit me in a dream that was so real it was like a vision. I saw him standing over us, his benign presence enough to reassure me, despite the absence of words.

CHAPTER TWENTY-THREE

Another Near Fatal Mistake

Once at home, we decided to boycott Dr. Schildwaechter, despite phone messages asking Jack to come in for an appointment and reminding us of our unpaid balance of $534.00. We had already paid thousands for this near-fatal treatment and Jack was not about to send him any more money. "Why should I when the bastard would have killed me?"

But Dr. Schildwaechter pressed on through a collection agency. Jack wrote to him detailing the suffering we had both endured from the vitamin A poisoning and his neglect to monitor Jack's liver function. Finally, when Dr. Schildwaechter threatened to take us to court, we engaged a lawyer who wrote to his lawyer saying that Dr. Schildwaechter "would be well advised not to pursue this matter" against Jack, and asking him to call. Our lawyer never received such a call.

However, Jack didn't want to see any more conventional medical types either. So he settled on another alternative doctor, Dr. Amim, an Iranian physician, who immediately took him off Aldactone, the diuretic that Dr. Scheef had prescribed in Germany. Dr. Amim maintained that Aldactone was much too harsh and might damage his liver further. So, he put Jack on an herbal diuretic—another mistake that turned out to be nearly fatal.

Everything was all right for a few weeks, but then Jack started losing strength again. He also started to have another disturbing physical symptom: he was retaining fluid to such an extent that he looked pregnant. Dr. Amim diagnosed it as ascites, fluid retention, and it seemed that his body was unable to get rid of the fluid through his kidneys. At night, Jack coughed and gagged so much that we both had trouble sleeping. Living with this huge belly was so uncomfortable that he was determined to have his stomach tapped. However, Dr. Amim didn't want to do it. Finally, Jack found a reluctant doctor in residency at a nearby hospital to do it–yet another big mistake. After the procedure, Jack's swollen belly returned to normal size, but he began to lose strength even more rapidly. Later, we found out that tapping these fluids, especially all at once, can lead to a serious loss of electrolytes and important minerals, putting great stress on the body's equilibrium.

Jack's body certainly showed the stress. His muscles twitched and jerked, and one night we thought he was having a heart attack. I rushed him to the E.R. at nearby Holy Cross Hospital where we waited for hours until a sympathetic resident examined him and asked a lot of questions about alcohol. When we told the young doctor about the massive doses of vitamin A, he was not surprised about the symptoms. It wasn't a heart attack, so we returned home with no treatment recommendations, much to my chagrin. We were going from crisis to crisis with no resolution.

After that, Jack made an appointment with Dr. Gold, who had originally referred him to the esophageal cancer protocol at NIH. When Dr. Gold found out that Dr. Amin had treated Jack, he refused to have anything to do with Jack because he didn't want his reputation compromised by association with Dr. Amim. We had little information about Dr. Amim, except that he was well known in alternative medical circles and he had patients who liked him. Later, I learned that the local medical board withdrew Dr. Amim's license to practice for two and one-half years for mishandling the care of several patients. But at this point, we sorely lacked information and guidance. I felt as though we were in a kind of purgatory between conventional and alternative medicine, unable to play by the rules of either. I was beginning to panic.

A week after the trip to the E.R. at Holy Cross, Jack awoke in the middle of the night breathless and twitching, with numbness and tingling moving up his legs. This time I took him to the E.R. at George Washington University Hospital in D.C. Again, a long wait to see the doctor on duty, and again, questions about alcohol, but we stressed the vitamin A overdose. By this time, Jack was fed up with the implications about alcoholism. After all, he had given up drinking nearly a year earlier. He became crabby and uncooperative, refusing a chest x-ray because he saw no reason for it. I desperately wanted suggestions for his treatment, but the doctor offered none. When I asked the doctor what to do and if we should perhaps go to the Mayo Clinic, he said, "You can do that if you want."

After that, I was determined to look for proper medical help and made an emergency appointment for Jack with my new internist, Dr. Rhinegold. Later, Dr. Rhinegold confessed to me that when he saw Jack, he was convinced he was looking at a man who was about to meet his maker. Dr. Rhinegold started Jack back on Aldactone and also put him on Lasix, a commonly used drug for treating fluid retention. After a few days, he referred Jack to a liver specialist, Dr. O'Keefe, who agreed to see him immediately and put Jack on a heavy dose of Lasix.

Jack liked and trusted Dr. O'Keefe, who made himself available by phone night and day. At this point, Jack had stopped seeing Dr. Amim. I did call Dr. O'Keefe more than once, very concerned for Jack's life. He told me that if Jack continued to deteriorate, he would have him hospitalized. By this time, Jack weighed 110 pounds, as opposed to his usual 140. His complexion was sallow, his eyes sunken, and his cheeks hollow. His speech was labored, and he didn't always make sense.

Why none of the doctors recommended putting Jack in the hospital and treating him like a dying patient who could be saved, I'll never know. It was as if the stigma of alternative medical care had made him a pariah. Or perhaps it was that they viewed him as an alcoholic who had destroyed his own liver, and therefore, his life was not all that valuable. Later, when Jack recovered, he used to remark that after all those years of drinking, his liver had remained remarkably intact, only to be nearly destroyed by vitamin A.

Although we both eventually returned to allopathic medicine, his treatment by much of the Washington D.C. medical establishment left us soured for many years. We also understood that alternative medicine had failed him just as badly, if not worse in this case. In the 1980s, there was a deep divide between mainstream and alternative medicine, with neither side willing to cooperate with the other. Fortunately, the situation has changed considerably, although we still have a long way to go. Nowadays, at least there is less mistrust and certainly less overt hostility between the two communities. In fact, some of the most well-known medical centers offer programs to complement their allopathic treatments, such as mediation, biofeedback, nutrition, acupuncture, and counseling.

Barbara knew that we were going through a crisis and made herself available to see us on a moment's notice. She must have seen how thin and gaunt he had become, but even she didn't see, at least at first, what was happening to Jack's mind as well as his body.

In the midst of this ordeal, Jack had begun to stay up late at night writing his obituary. He saw nothing creepy about it and said it was good for him. He called it "obit therapy." Then he started to get strange fixations. One night, he accused me of delaying his dinner purposefully so as to make him late for his Reiki appointment. He became cranky and aggressive with his friends as well as with me. He would get up in the middle of the night and write letters, telling everybody how to clean up their act, then he would sleep for hours during the day. Because he fell asleep at the wheel one time, I started to do all the driving. I increased our acupressure sessions. By this time, Jack was unable to do anything around the house, so I did all the shopping, cooking, and housework in addition to my consulting practice.

That December my father visited to give me some moral support. During his visit, there was an episode where I felt so exasperated by Jack's lack of ability to do anything around the house that I lashed out at him. My father gently chided me for my temper and pointed out how sick Jack really was. I was ashamed.

During this period, we kept going to our group therapy appointments, even though Jack looked like he was at death's door. When I complained about *my* lot, one of the women in the group called me a whiny bitch. After that, I refused to go to the group, but Barbara made the woman call me and apologize. Once again, I hauled myself back over to Barbara's house.

Although I hated the group at that moment, I knew I needed Barbara's support, and I felt inadequate to the argument that would ensue if I flat-out quit.

At one point, Jack became extremely annoyed with Barbara for not taking proper care of her BMW. When he called her at 2:00 a.m. to tell her that the chrome on her wheels had become pitted because she didn't wash them regularly, she got the picture. She told Jack that we should both come in the next day for an appointment. Finally, I was able to unburden myself with someone who understood exactly what was happening. My husband had become a stranger, peculiar and sometimes hostile, and was dying. My world, despite my best efforts, was coming apart.

For several weeks, Jack struggled with his obituary and with his failing body. It was as if he were suspended between life and death. He kept taking the Lasix, and I plodded ahead with daily practicalities. The only event that I can remember was a severe January snowstorm that would have left us marooned, but our next-door neighbor, David, and his two little boys shoveled our driveway and our front walk without so much as a word. Even now, I want to cry when I think about that act of kindness. But as the storm passed, and the sun came out on the glistening snow and the clear drive, Jack began to feel just a little better. At last, we started to believe that the crisis might be over. It was Martin Luther King's birthday.

Little by little, day-by-day, Jack began to gain strength. He finally let go of his obituary, and within just a few weeks he had gained much of the lost weight and returned to his normal, cheerful self. We had made it, thanks to the Lasix and the extraordinary healing power of his body. And, for all we knew, thanks to the spirits who were hovering over us, despite our ignorance of their presence. There were no more midnight trips to the hospital, no more visits either to Dr. Amim or Dr. Schildwaechter, and of course, no more goddamned vitamin A.

We continued our therapy sessions with Barbara for another year, even the group therapy, somewhat reluctantly. Somehow, we knew that the hardest part was over. If Jack could survive two death sentences from cancer and near death from vitamin A poisoning, and I could survive the whole ordeal by his side, we knew we would make it through most anything.

Later that year, we gave ourselves a trip to Hawaii's sunny beaches and soft air as a reward. Then we flew on to South Korea for a few days of sightseeing and to shop for the exquisite Korean celadon ceramics with its pale, jade-green glaze. From there, I went on alone to China for a professional meeting in Beijing and a post-meeting group tour. Jack thought it was all a great idea. Two weeks of green tea, a climb up the Great Wall, and floating down the Yangtze River. At last, a brand new adventure and the beginning of a new life with cancer in the distant past, never to return.

CHAPTER TWENTY-FOUR
The Healing

People often ask what it was that actually healed Jack. What was the key ingredient?

I reply that I don't know and will never know. It could have happened right at the end of the Janker Klinik's treatment and at the beginning of our forays into the alternative world with Frau Anni's healing.

Or, it could have been the arduous months of psychotherapy with Barbara and Jack's other therapy groups.

Or perhaps the key ingredients were all the bodywork and the many months of acupressure and foot reflexology, Reiki, Johrei, and massage—and later, the absence of alcohol. All of this might have helped, in addition to Jack's daily practice of meditation and visualization.

Some have suggested that it was the year of vitamin A overdose acting as a kind of low-level, prolonged chemotherapy. That could be, but the psychic Christine pronounced the cancer gone when Jack was just a few weeks into the vitamin A regimen. Then again, our concept of time, and the strict divisions between past, present, and future, can be quite different from a psychic's perspective.

Certainly, Jack's strong body and steadfast determination to live must have played a part, as well as his coming to terms with all the disappointments and deaths he had experienced up to that point. Or, it could have been a combination of any or all of these.

Exactly when the healing took place and what caused it was relatively unimportant to us, since the overriding importance was his cure. Certainly, it would be good to know which activity was the definitive one, if that were the case. Everyone yearns for the magic bullet that has so successfully eluded the cancer research community for all these years. But as I survey all the interlocking steps of this drama, I can't help but see the guiding hand of something far greater than each of us.

One thing for certain is that is that over the course of those two years, Jack changed. Both of us changed. Of necessity, we became open to life's many possibilities, both of us becoming more aware of our spiritual and intuitive sides, and more loving and accepting of ourselves, and one another. Jack even reconciled with his stepmother with whom he hadn't communicated for decades. Although he didn't actually visit her, he initiated a correspondence that the two of them carried out until her death a few years later. Her relatives told us that she was thrilled that Jack had accepted her back into his life.

Jack knew the cancer and its fallout were actually gifts for which he was grateful, calling it his "cosmic kick in the ass." He believed that good cancer counseling was not only a blessing but a right to which every cancer patient should be entitled. In a letter to the editor of the *Washington Post*, published Sept. 30, 1986, Jack wrote the following:

> From my experience this past year, I know that the type of counseling that emphasizes the patient's role in his recovery can be invaluable. It can help get rid of the anger, anxiety, and depression that played havoc with the immune system in the first place; replace passivity with hope and action; and in general, improve one's outlook on life. In fact, there is no doubt in my mind that this part of my treatment was more important than all of the radiation and chemotherapy I received, which ultimately was ineffective. It's too bad it took me three years to find this out. It's much, much worse that many never do.

Jack often acknowledged his own role in the formation of his cancer—excessive drinking and years of smoking, compounded by years of stored anger and grief. He saw how these toxic ingredients set him up for damage, specifically to his esophagus. At the same time, we both agreed that a blame-the-victim attitude was not only unhelpful but could be harmful. Any New-Age advice like "improve your attitude" or "examine how you did this to yourself" will often backfire, leaving the patient emotionally desolate as well as sick. Jack did feel that acknowledging his own role in bringing on the disease helped him to combat it. Certainly, he never asked "Why me?" because he was quite sure of the answer.

I agreed with Jack's assessment but felt that it was more complicated. Everyone is different. For me, the key would be paying close attention to one's body and one's feelings—then acceptance, not resignation. Acceptance of the disease and any emotional component is crucial, and then getting help to deal with it. Also, acceptance of the very real possibility of death, which will claim us all eventually.

I, too, experienced many benefits from this ordeal. Accepting my own failings helped me to be more comfortable in my own skin and more loving toward others. I learned to embrace my shadow as the Jungians would say, acknowledging its juice as well as its less acceptable aspects. The reassurance I gained from Barbara, as well as from Jack and others, helped me to understand that anger toward the cancer victim was normal and understandable, and that expressing it in the therapeutic situation enabled me to keep from acting it out. Better for Jack and better for me. Not only was I able to accept "the bitch within," but to harness her energy in productive ways.

I would never go so far as to say that cancer is always a blessing, as it can surely be a tragedy. But it can definitely be an important wake-up call, a valuable opening. It can be, as it was with us, the cosmic kick we both needed.

Epilogue

By 1988, Washington, D.C. had begun to lose its luster. After seven years of Ronald Reagan, the city was teeming with lobbyists, and the government programs we had each worked so hard to build had begun to be dismantled. Jack's children had been launched into the world–Marianne was well established at Virginia Commonwealth University and Rob was about to start at the University of Maryland–so the nest was pretty much empty. Despite the fact that Jack had always maintained his identity as an "East Coast Boy," we began to think about moving.

I was pushing for the West Coast, but then I was offered a job in Cincinnati working for the National Institute for Occupational Safety and Health. Since I had lived near Dayton for two years doing the research for my doctoral dissertation, my first reaction was "no thank you, I've had enough of Ohio." But Jack liked Cincinnati, having traveled there often when he worked for the Public Health Service, and I liked the people with whom I would be working. So, we decided to give Cincinnati a try, at least for a while.

We sold our house in suburban Maryland, said good-bye to our friends, and moved that December. It was five years after we had begun this cancer journey, and nearly two years after that snowy day in January when Jack's victory over vitamin A poisoning began to manifest. We no longer had any doubts about Jack's health.

This time, I was only able to tolerate the government bureaucracy less than two years, and I went right back to my consulting practice. Jack made furniture in his makeshift shop in the basement and volunteered for a nonprofit concerned with inner-city housing. Since he was truly retired and I was working full time, Jack did all the shopping and cooking, and I relished being taken care of so well.

While Jack had previously disdained anything that smacked of organized religion, he became an ardent churchgoer at the Unity New Thought Center in Cincinnati. Unity's open-minded, non-dogmatic approach to spirituality appealed to him, as did the emphasis on taking responsibility for our lives. Unity teaches that we create our life experiences through our way of thinking, and hence, the importance of switching from negative to positive. Jack was always sure to get me up and out of the house on Sunday morning in time for the ten o'clock service.

We made lasting friendships at Unity, where we established a serious illness support group. It had started as a cancer support group, but at the first meeting a man with AIDS came in, and so we changed our name. We would always start with meditation and guided imagery, and then just talk. But the talk was not about doctors and chemotherapy as much as it was about people's feelings, challenges, and supplemental practices, like acupressure, Reiki, and the Chinese movement practices of tai chi and Qigong. In fact, one of our participants opened a store with various kinds of healing classes, books, and accessories, and called it the "Whatever Works Wellness Center." As of 2014, the store is still doing a thriving business. Many members of our healing group have not survived, but some have, and others lived long beyond their prognoses. We treasured the resulting relationships.

Our long-range dream had been to move to Ashland, Oregon. We had read about it in a book called *Retirement Choices*, and friends had recommended this charming little Oregon city near California's border. Although we had intended to look at various places in Oregon and Northern California on our exploratory trip to the West Coast, as soon as we saw Ashland, we knew this would be our new home.

Due to the combination of good friends, Unity Church, and our inertia, we lingered three more years in Cincinnati. Finally, in summer 1993 we moved into our lovely new house in Ashland with a view of the valley and mountains beyond. It was easy to settle into small-city life with a highly educated population and so much culture. Ashland was home to the Oregon Shakespeare

Festival, which ran from February to November, in addition to good music and art.

Even when we lived in Cincinnati, Jack had dreamed of opening an art gallery. We had been building our own collection of fine art prints for many years, which included woodblock prints, lithographs, and etchings. We both felt that prints were the best choice for people who wanted beautiful art from accomplished artists at an affordable price. Jack's experience with art in Germany—both the good and the bad—was critical to his dream. He strongly believed in the healing power of beauty, and he wanted to help bring that beauty into people's lives.

Once settled in Ashland, we opened "Graven Images Gallery," and soon after, Jack co-founded the Ashland Gallery Association. He also rekindled "A Taste of Ashland," an annual art and wine festival. Jack's new passion was to promote the arts in Ashland every way he could. Our gallery specialized in printmakers and ceramicists from the Pacific Northwest. Although a lot of our art found good homes, the gallery was, as Jack said, "a critical success and a commercial failure." We had given ourselves three years in which to break even financially, but it just didn't happen, so we closed in 1997.

I think of the gallery as just one of the several activities in which Jack engaged as a form of sharing with others some of the benefits that had come to him from his great gift of healing. Whether it was community service in the inner city of Cincinnati, building expertly crafted furniture for people's homes, or creating a gallery that offered fine art to enrich their lives—all of these efforts were ways to give back to humanity. This seems to be characteristic of people who have had such a dramatic reprieve and a second chance at life.

I kept on with my consulting practice with the aid of email, telephone, and occasional business trips, but started working less and enjoying the benefits of Ashland more. The community was rich with cultural opportunities: poetry workshops, theater, and chamber music concerts, just to name a few. I started a weekly writing group with several women friends, a creative and nurturing activity that continued throughout my years in Ashland. Our dog Max loved the hiking trails, and Jack's kids shared some Christmases and other family times with us. Marianne referred to our new home as "Spa Ashland."

Our beloved Max lived to be almost fourteen, relatively old for a Labrador. Once while I was on a business trip, Jack called to say that Max was not doing well and the vet had recommended surgery. I flew home right away. As Max was waiting for what would be her final surgery, I sat with her and the veterinary technician and talked about how she had seen us through two episodes of "terminal" cancer, near death from the treatment fallout, and the healing of a troubled marriage. I told how she had languished at home while we spent months in Germany, how she endured our fights and our tears, taking on our burdens as if she bore the responsibility. Patient and forgiving to the end, Max's open heart was a model for all. We both wept as we stroked her silky coat. It was our last time together. She didn't survive the surgery.

Once the gallery closed, Jack was drawn to city politics just as he had been to national politics in Washington. It was as if "Potomac Fever" never really left his system, although Ashland politics were hardly as grand as the inner circle Jack had been part of. He was a natural, behind-the-scenes guy, and he persuaded some of his many friends to start looking into certain dysfunctional elements of Ashland's city government. He became quite popular with many of Ashland's progressive population, as well as unpopular with some of the city's more entrenched residents who preferred the status quo.

In 2003, Jack decided to run for the Ashland City Council. In fact, our friends had suggested that I be the one to run, and Jack very much liked the idea so he could keep on being the mover and shaker behind the scenes. But when I saw how nasty it could be, I refused. So he decided to do it. Jack ran an excellent campaign and won handily, after which he became caught up in the ordinary struggles endemic to governing. Soon it became clear that his energy and morale were affected by this new job. The council was seriously divided, the mayor seemed unable to provide effective leadership, and Jack's most cherished project, the creation of a downtown master plan, foundered.

However, life was good in many ways during this time. We saw both children happily married—Marianne in 2002 and Robert in 2004. Despite the rigors of the city's budget season, I persuaded Jack to go to Central Europe in May 2004, and together, we explored Budapest, Bratislava, and Prague. Each time we arrived in a new city, he found the closest Internet cafe so he could keep track of the Ashland City Council's activities.

During Jack's tenure on the council, I felt as though his stamina was beginning to decline. His doctor detected some cardiac irregularities and recommended a pacemaker, which was eventually installed. Jack had suffered from sleep apnea for months and was taking oxygen at night, but the doctors didn't recommend any other kind of treatment for it. Somehow, that made me nervous, and I suggested a re-evaluation, but that never took place.

Everything seemed to be going all right, well enough that I could go to England on a long-planned trip to visit my cousins in London and a nephew in Cambridge. I could also indulge my passion for chamber music, both at Wigmore Hall in London and at a festival in Chipping Camden. I had left my itinerary and telephone numbers with Jack. Although I called and talked to him once, the rest of the time I was only able to leave messages on the answering machine. One day, I visited the library in Chipping Camden to check my email and received a raft of terrifying messages: "Call your niece." "Call John

Stromberg." And "I'm so sorry to hear the bad news." Nothing saying, "Call home."

I rushed back to my B&B and called Jack's friend John Stromberg. John had worried about Jack when he didn't hear from him after two days. On Tuesday, John saw the Sunday *New York Times* still in the driveway, and found his way into the house through the back deck. Jack had died in his sleep that Sunday night, the oxygen machine still going, and our dog and cat in a state of agitation. John said Jack looked incredibly peaceful.

It took two days for people to find me because Jack was the only one with my itinerary, and it was buried in his in-box. My cousin Frances had driven to Chipping Camden from London, going from hotel to hotel trying to find me. The police had been doing likewise. They all converged around the same time. Frances stayed with me that evening, offering to spend the night, but somehow I wanted to be alone with my grief.

Those few days must have been the worst in my life. Unlike the condition of many survivors of a spouse's death, nothing was a blur. I remember every detail; the fierce pain, the total inability to sleep, the regret for having left him alone, the desolation after my friends had dropped me off at Heathrow, and the near panic at being confined in an airplane for so many hours. I also remember so clearly the outpouring of support and affection from friends everywhere.

Once I reached Ashland, my beloved family traveled to be with me. Rob and his wife, Lori, had already arrived, and Marianne and her husband, Patrick, soon followed, as did a contingent of Hardestys from Texas, and my niece Catherine. Many friends in Ashland planned and brought meals, sent flowers, wrote letters, and left candles on the doorstep.

I felt that an autopsy was unnecessary. It seemed clear that Jack was overcome by a massive heart attack. Exactly what kind of cardiovascular event didn't matter. His doctor explained that Jack's ordeal with cancer had probably weakened his heart. Added to that were the effects of many months of intense chemotherapy, four months of radiation, and nearly a year dealing with the toxic effects of vitamin A. Undoubtedly, all of this took its toll.

John's assessment of Jack's peaceful countenance when he discovered Jack that Tuesday seemed accurate. I could hardly believe how youthful and peaceful he looked. The funeral home had made no changes to his appearance. When I touched Jack's body it was cold, but his expression was warm and serene. His massage therapist, who was well acquainted with Jack's body, helped me wash him as a final blessing and good-bye.

More than one of Jack's friends suggested that he was ready to go. Although I have tried to resist the notion, I believe his peaceful demeanor meant that he didn't leave this life unwillingly. At first, I found that thought distressing, but after seeing his tranquil expression that

Saturday, I've had to admit that it could be true. There is the voice in me that cries, *How could you? After all we've been through and when we could still have such a good life!*

But those are unanswerable questions, along with so many others. Would he have lived longer if he had not had the stress and frustration of the Ashland City Council? Would I have suffered more, or perhaps suffered less, if we had not had all of the near-death experiences back in the mid 1980s? There is no way to know. For me, there is one question that *is* answerable. And that is whether Jack would have survived despite two "terminal" diagnoses some twenty years earlier if we *hadn't* done some of the things we did to support his healing. Exactly *which* things worked their magic remains a mystery.

I do know that my own attitude toward death has been forever changed. Although I appreciate my life and intend to keep on with it for several more years, in good health I hope, I have little fear of death. No doubt one reason is all of the uncanny spiritual experiences we both had during our healing in the 1980s. It was as if, as the ancient Celts would say, the veil between the worlds of spirit and matter, between heaven and earth, became extremely thin and porous, allowing us a glimpse of the mysterious universe that is far beyond our ordinary world.

If Frau Anni Ziemer could cause a palpable column of energy to rise above Jack's head, if Dr. Lang could return fifty years after his own death to heal patients through the medium of George Chapman, if Gaye Muir could make such supremely plausible identifications of the spirits hovering around Jack, then what else is going on out there? What about the people who walk through walls? What about the solid citizens who encounter angels? Sometimes, I feel as though we are ants crawling around on blades of grass, completely ignorant of the realm of giants—little beings who have no concept of the vast universe beyond our immediate spheres of comprehension.

A few years after Jack's death, I vacationed in Brazil with my brother and sister-in-law. We stayed in a hotel in Salvador that happened to be right next door to a Johrei center. So I worked up the courage to ring the bell and a portly, dark-skinned woman answered. Although I spoke virtually no Portuguese, I was able to use the word *marito* for husband, and then I put my hand on my heart and started to cry. She guided me into a softly lit room, seated me in the lone chair in the middle, and held her hands close to my body in the traditional Johrei healing. After a while she left, and a young man came in and performed the same ritual. No explanation was necessary or even possible for the tears that never stopped until I said my *obrigada* (thanks) and left. I longed to share this experience with Jack, to tell him that I had found the Johrei practitioners in this huge Brazilian city right next door to my hotel, and that they had given me a treatment without needing any spoken communication. Then I realized that I didn't have to tell him because he was there.

Photos

*Jack Hardesty in 1978, about four years
before his cancer diagnosis.*

Jack's children in 1979, around the time we married.
Marianne was eleven and Rob was nine.

Alice and the loyal family dog, Max, in 1984.

*From left, Jack, fellow patient Fanny, her husband, Rocky,
and Alvin, patient John's partner, from the Janker Klinik.
We were out for an evening on the town in Bonn,
summer 1985.*

Our German friends and teachers, Udo and Anke, with Jack and me (second from left) at our hotel in Bonn, October 1986. They were a great support to us during our healing journey in Germany.

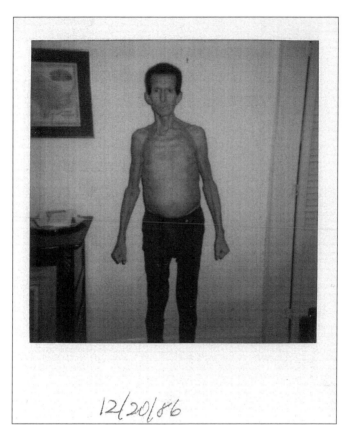

Jack at the worst of his Vitamin A poisoning
in December 1986. This treatment nearly killed him.

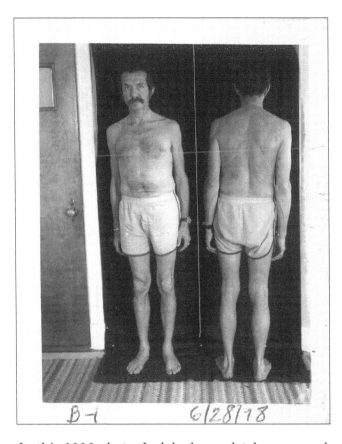

*In this 1998 photo, Jack had completely recovered
from cancer twelve years earlier.*

Jack's grown children in October 1998, Marianne and Rob, celebrating Jack's 70th birthday at a party in Washington D.C.

Resources

During the last thirty years, there has been a burgeoning of resources in complementary and alternative medicine, so much so that you will sometimes see it referred to simply as CAM. The following is an overview.

Psychoneuroimmunology

The importance of the body-mind connection, which our ancestors intuitively understood long before Hippocrates, gained a wider understanding and popularity in modern medicine when the word and concept "psychoneuroimmunology" appeared in the scientific literature in 1975. Its lengthy title reflects a complex interdisciplinary approach to health and illness, and the influence of the nervous system on the immune system that incorporates the disciplines of psychology, physiology, neuroscience, genetics, pharmacology, molecular biology, and several other fields.

In the mid-20th century, Hans Selye elucidated the body-mind relationship, demonstrating through his research the effect of stress on the immune system. In 1981, researchers Robert Ader, Nicholas Cohen, and David Felton published the book, *Psychoneuroimmunology,* which put forward considerable scientific evidence on how the brain and immune system work together so intimately.

About the time my husband, Jack Hardesty, was going through treatment at the National Cancer Institute, neuro-scientist and pharmacologist Candace Pert was doing research at NIH and established the close connection between neuropeptides, emotions, and the immune system. At the time, I remember how controversial it sounded, but now the concept of psychoneuroimmunology and the mind-body connection has become generally accepted worldwide.

Complementary and Alternative Medicine

Today, Western medicine doctors are often open to adjunctive programs such as meditation, stress reduction, diet, and counseling, as long as they complement traditional allopathic treatments with chemotherapy, surgery, and radiation. The extent to which traditional doctors recommend–or even tolerate–less traditional approaches will vary among allopathic physicians or medical centers. Some MDs may welcome a variety of complementary treatments such as acupuncture, herbal medicines and supplements, yoga, and spiritual healing, while many others are passively skeptical, and some who adamantly discourage these treatments. Usually, these treatments fall into the category of "unproven"–which, in itself is debatable considering recent scientific research. To the extreme, some conservative doctors would even discourage prayer as fostering "false hope"! The fear in the medical community is that patients will select alternative practices *instead* of allopathic medicine, and hence, the medical community's distaste for the word "alternative."

However, allopathic physicians are increasingly inclined to work with patients to develop a holistic program based on the individual patient's needs and desires. Treating the whole person with "integrative medicine" is a welcome improvement over the either/or situation that Jack and I encountered thirty years ago. Today, it could mean a growing assortment of contemporary oncological treatments for cancer combined with any of the following: chiropractic, exercise and fitness, stress reduction, smoking cessation, nutrition programs that include vitamins, herbs, and supplements, homeopathy, naturopathic medicine, psychotherapy, energy medicine, acupuncture, acupressure, massage, music and art therapy, biofeedback, yoga, tai chi, and Qigong. Some of these treatments may even be paid for by insurance.

The following list of resources is a sample of those I have found interesting and useful. New resources are becoming available all the time, especially on the Internet. I encourage readers to do their own Internet searches, ask their health care providers for suggestions, and check with the libraries of hospitals and cancer centers.

Integrative Cancer Centers

Even some of the most conventional medical centers now provide complementary services. The Society for Integrative Oncology (SIO), formed in 2003, states as its mission to advance evidence-based, comprehensive, integrative healthcare for people affected by cancer. The idea is to empower patients and their families to become active participants in their own care. Among the well-established institutions listed by the SIO are programs at:

—MD Anderson Cancer Center, Houston, Texas
—Memorial Sloan-Kettering Cancer Center, New York, New York
—Winship Cancer Institute, Emory University, Atlanta, Georgia
—Dana-Farber Cancer Institute, Boston, Massachusetts
—Juravinski Cancer Centre at McMaster University, Hamilton, Ontario, Canada
—Block Center for Integrative Cancer Treatment, Skokie, Illinois

One of the pioneers in integrative medicine is Keith Block, M.D., who, with his wife Penny Block, Ph.D., founded their center in 1980. The Block Center treats the entire range of cancers, combining conventional cancer treatments, including innovative molecular treatments and immunotherapies, along with complementary programs in nutrition and supplements, body-mind training, exercise instruction, and counseling. Programs are tailored to each individual patient. The center is also a teaching and research institution for medical, nutrition, and pharmacy students.

Books

Cancer as a Turning Point: A Handbook for People with Cancer, Their Families, and Health Professionals. LeShan, Lawrence, Ph.D. (Plume, 1990, 1994).

The Cancer Fighting Kitchen: Nourishing, Big-Flavor Recipes for Cancer Treatment and Recovery. Katz, Rebecca & Edelson, Max (Ten Speed Press, 2010).

Close to the Bone: Life-Threatening Illness as a Soul Journey. Bolen, Jean Shinoda, M.D. (Conari Press,1996, 2007).

Choices in Healing: Integrating the Best of Conventional and Complementary Approaches to Cancer. Lerner, Michael, Ph.D. (The MIT Press, 1994, 1996).

Fire in the Soul: A New Psychology of Spiritual Optimism. Borysenko, Joan, Ph.D. (Grand Central Publishing, 1993, 2001).

Getting Well Again: A Step-by-Step, Self-Help Guide to Overcoming Cancer for Patients and Their Families. Simonton, O. Carl, M.D., Mathews-Simonton, Stephanie, & Creighton, James (Bantam, 1978, 1992).

Imagery in Healing: Shamanism and Modern Medicine. Achterberg, Jeanne, Ph.D. (Shambhala,1985, 2002).

Kitchen Table Wisdom. Remen, Rachel Naomi, M.D. (Penguin 1996, 2006).

Life Over Cancer: The Block Center Program for Integrative Cancer Treatment. Block, Keith I., M.D. (Bantam, 2009).

Radical Remission: Surviving Cancer Against All Odds. Turner, Kelly, Ph.D. (HarperOne, 2014).

Organizations

Annie Appleseed Project: This organization provides extensive information about cancer clinics, cancer types, and complementary and alternative treatments. The project hosts periodic conferences.

Caring Bridge: Web-based organization that facilitates communication between patients undergoing treatment and their families and friends.

Healing Journeys: A national program sponsoring periodic workshops and no-cost conferences for patients, family members, and professionals called "Cancer as a Turning Point." Other workshops include "The Cancer-Fighting Kitchen" and "Sexy After Cancer." Topics primarily concern complementary and alternative healing. This program also provides a monthly newsletter, DVDs, and CDs from conferences and workshops. Healing retreats to Mexico are also available.

CDs and Audio Books

Cancer as a Turning Point: From Surviving to Thriving (Sounds True 2007). This is a two-volume set of audio recordings from the Healing Journeys conferences. This CD set features several bestselling authors and healers, many of whom are thriving after cancer diagnoses. They reframe the healing process in a positive, creative, spiritual light, as well as discuss complementary and alternative cancer treatments. Authors include Jean Shinoda Bolen, Jeanne Achterberg, Joan Borysenko, Michael Lerner, Wayne Muller, Lawrence LeShan, Rachel Naomi Remen, and more.

Meditation to Help You Fight Cancer by Belleruth Naparstek. (Health Journeys 1991). Meditation and guided imagery combines images of shrinking tumors and fighter cells triumphing over cancer cells.

Meditations for Personal Healing by Louise Hay (Hay House 1995). This CD by the best-selling author of *You Can Heal Your Life* offers guided meditations promoting healing by inspiring relaxation and the reminder of beauty in everyday life.

Recovery Programs and Retreats

Cancer as a Turning Point: Five-day residential workshops presented by Lawrence LeShan, Ph.D, Ruth Bolletino, Ph.D., and Mary Bobis, LCSW. These workshops are for patients and their families challenged by cancer or other illnesses involving the immune system. There is an emphasis on adding richness and zest to life. Workshops take place at various locations nationally,

Commonweal: This health and environmental research institute in Bolinas, California offers weeklong residential retreats at the Commonweal Cancer Help Program. The healing program includes group support sessions, massage, yoga, meditation, imagery work, poetry, and symbolic learning exercises.

Simonton Cancer Center: Founded more than forty years ago by O. Carl Simonton, M.D., in Santa Barbara, California. The Simonton method focuses on interactions between the mind and the body, and how beliefs, attitudes, lifestyle choices, spiritual and psychological perspectives can dramatically affect our health, the course of our disease, and our overall well-being. Five-day workshops are based on the method pioneered in the book *Getting Well Again,* which focuses on interactions between mind and body.

Smith Center for Healing and the Arts: Based in Washington, D.C., the retreats are for people facing a life-threatening illness. The retreats can last one, three, or seven days. They include various integrative and complementary therapies with the option to explore healing through the arts.

About the Author

Alice Hardesty is a poet and writer whose work has been published in several journals. She is also a social, environmental, and political activist, working to protect the planet for future generations. In her other life as Alice H. Suter, Ph.D., she is principal of her consulting firm, Alice Suter & Associates, which specializes in understanding and preventing the adverse effects of occupational and environmental noise.

Alice Hardesty and Bacho

In this capacity she has authored several monographs and technical publications. Hardesty lives in Portland, Oregon with her dog, Bacho, and her cat, Wabi Sabi. *An Uncommon Cancer Journey* is her first book.

www.bachopress.com

Bacho 🌀 *Press*

Made in the USA
San Bernardino, CA
15 August 2014